"MOVE OVER"
students, politics, religion

"MOVE OVER"

students, politics, religion

FRANCIS CARLING

SHEED AND WARD : NEW YORK

© *Sheed and Ward, Inc., 1969*

Library of Congress Catalog Card Number 69-19252

Manufactured in the United States of America

For Elisabeth Morse Kelley,
without whom this book would
have been much more possible.

contents

foreword
the "cool" generation?   9

1 a new generation   21

2 the classroom crisis   39

3 from politics to the movement   67

4 religion and rebellion   89

5 the sectarianism of the movement   115

6 the sensibilities of the movement   135

conclusion
student power and hope   151

foreword

the "cool" generation?

In the Spring of 1967, six students gathered at the Williams Club in Manhattan at the invitation of *Commonweal* magazine to discuss student attitudes toward religion. All the students were or had been Catholics, and each was attending, or had attended, a Catholic college. They had been invited because they represented a fair cross section of today's "activist" students. Their common background seemed to promise that the discussion would merely be a repetitious attack on the church by six identical rebels. As it turned out, the talk was spirited and disagreement among the participants general. *Commonweal* tape-recorded several hours of the discussion and published it in their October 6, 1967 issue as a symposium entitled, "The Cool Generation and the Church." This book is *not* that symposium, although it was occasioned by it.

The participants were: Martha Ann Brazier from Boston College and Mary Frances Campion from Rosary College and Temple University, who represented perhaps the most typical kind of Catholic student activist—well-informed, eager for reform and willing to work for change within the church despite its failings; John Burke, Jr., a Jesuit seminarian who had studied at Holy Cross, Boston College and Northwestern, and who was frustrated and indignant about the church in a way that only one professionally committed to its service could be; Kathy McHale from Newton College of the Sacred Heart and Stanford, who was several years older than the others and was most concerned with the paradox of fighting against the very traditions, American and Catholic, which had formed her; William Wilson from LaSalle College in Philadelphia, who had dropped out of the church and America long ago; and myself, from Fordham College and Yale Law School.

What became apparent from the discussion was that it is not possible for such a group of students to discuss their religion without discussing politics. When I read the published symposium the next fall, it occurred to me that the things we talked about were relevant to a larger discussion of politics and religion, despite our similarity of background and the fact that we had talked mainly about the Catholic Church. We had much to say but not enough. Although the discussion ventured away from intramural Catholic problems, it never stayed away very long. I left the discussion and read it later, feeling that much remained to be said. That feeling resulted in the writing of this book.

Commonweal chose to call the symposium "The Cool Generation and the Church," a title that still makes me wince. My generation is anything but "cool." The era when detachment was regarded as a virtue ended in 1960. My generation would be better described as "hot." Never before have so many young people been so embroiled in the process of social change. This book is an attempt to sketch and describe from two specific angles a part of the experience of that generation. It is about how it *feels* to be part of this new generation and concerned about religion and politics. But since "generations" do not in fact exist—as they might, if babies were born in convenient spurts every twenty-five years—it must be admitted at the outset that my point of departure is in some sense fictional.

Perhaps it is time to abandon the "generation" simplification altogether. Classifying the population into age clusters violates the continuity of change and growth. Generalizations about a narrowly defined age group become outdated almost as soon as they are formulated, since each "age group" is constantly becoming a different one, and individuals remain in one age group—except, possibly, "middle age"—scarcely long enough to register their impressions, let alone present conclusions based on them.

Still the notion of a "generation" is relevant, especially when we are speaking of young people in the 60's, because the members of this group are living through a unique experience —which is precisely the point to be demonstrated here—and because we are so easily located. We sit on campuses all across the country, going through our paces, awaiting and inviting inspection. We have, I think it fair to say, called a certain amount of attention to ourselves. Our participation in the civil rights and peace movements, attempts to change the policies of our universities and our life style that questions many of the standards of our society are in marked contrast to the behavior of our predeccessors. Youth will not; it cannot be ignored.

Why do I speak of "my generation" as though it really had a distinct existence? In what ways are young adults today distinguishable from other age groups? Has our experience really been unique?

My generation is distinguishable, first of all, because those on the threshold of adulthood are always different from their elders. Although we are old enough to have a vision of how things should be, we are too young to achieve it. This breeds distinct social, political and religious attitudes. To a young man at college, life seems a game in which older men hold all the cards and will only reluctantly deal him in. There is some question whether this is really the case, however. The way the major parties selected presidential candidates in 1968 certainly leaves room for doubt whether the average American of any age wields much political influence. Nevertheless, young people *feel* powerless and most other Americans do not, though more and more are beginning to share our feeling. This feeling of powerlessness accounts for the often frantic, and sometimes desperate, forms that our political expression takes.

To this anxiety must be added, of course, the willingness of the young and unmarried to take risks that men and women with families and careers dare not take. There is no point in belaboring the obvious truth that conservatism often ripens with age or to attempt to attack or justify such "evolution." Radical thinking and experimentation do come more naturally to those who expect to live so long that they can afford to sit out a period of disruption and rapid change in the hope of enjoying its fruits much later.

So much could have been said of any "young generation" at any time. All that has been pointed out so far is that the student generation of today is unlike its elders just as students always have been. It is different in exactly the way that our elders were different when they were students. However, my colleagues and our elders are separated by a wider chasm than the ordinary generation gap. The atom bomb radically changed the process of rebellion and eventual absorption which has always characterized coming into manhood. New ideas—change for change's sake—have always been a favorite of the young, but, as in the matter of beards, such rebellion often has only symbolic worth. It is little more than emotional and psychic calisthenics.

The atomic bomb, however, has rendered change absolutely imperative. Old politics and ideologies, all the old attitudes, have brought us to the brink of destruction. To the many who have become numb to the threat of nuclear war this might seem hyperbolic dramatizing; no one hears many students agitating over atomic weapons stockpiling these days, or at least not with the intensity with which they confront other issues. But the Bomb—an incredibly real danger in itself— symbolizes the immense potential for violence that many of our "traditional" problems have recently assumed. Racial ferment in this country, to cite the most glaring example, is nothing like what it ever was before. It is not just our old problem intensified; it has taken on an aura of immediacy and danger that cry for a solution now. The "older generation" will have to do some of the solving, but we expect it to establish only a truce, if anything at all. Lasting racial peace, which means racial justice in our society, can be created only by the young, whose hopes still outnumber their fears.

In many ways, of course, the "generation gap" still takes the old form. The young accuse their elders of trying to meet new problems with old answers and of bringing the world to the brink of disaster. But the similarity in form should not be allowed to disguise the real difference in content. Today the

world *is* on the brink of disaster. Previously the worst damage
that old men could inflict on the world was, say, a World War
I; and they regularly did inflict it in many shapes and forms
because man never before really *had* to live with his neighbor.
Today the same vital problems encompass the globe: race,
poverty, population explosion. Each of these problems lures
man closer and closer to the expedient of nuclear war which
makes them not just larger versions of the old rivalries but
dangerously different. While every "younger generation" has
felt like remaking the world, this generation knows that it
must or suffer death—an awesome realization for a young
man unsure of his intellectual footing and inexperienced with
the tools of change. This book is concerned with the effects of
that realization upon the politics and religion of the members
of my generation who experienced it most powerfully.

I am concerned here with the intersection of politics and
religion. I use this approach because of my own interest in the
present and future condition of religion and because of my
strong conviction that politics and religion are inextricably
linked in the lives of today's students. This double concern
puts certain limits on my ability to generalize, for only a small
minority of student activists are conventionally religious, and
only a small minority of religious students are political or
religious activists. The group about which I shall be talking is
thus twice atypical, but this narrow position has its advantages. The religious activist stands in a position of singular
ability to criticize both the politics of his generation and the
failings of his church. One of the more striking demonstrations
of the accelerating irrelevance of institutional religion in this
country is that student activists do not much care for religious
criticism, and the church either ignores or attempts to suppress
its activists' pleas for reform. If the voice of the religious

student activist is one that no one wants to hear, it is nonetheless a voice of great importance for the church, even if the wilderness that it cries from happens sometimes to be politics.

I hope that this preoccupation with religion does not limit this book to a sectarian audience. I shall talk most often about Catholic students because my own religious background has been Catholic, since I was educated for sixteen years in Catholic schools. Also, a good deal of my political formation and activity has been among Catholics, and I find Catholicism intrinsically interesting and important. Despite my own strong reservations about the church, I see it as one of organized religion's better hopes in a world where religion is fragmented and is being pushed more and more into a back row of human experience. I would go so far as to hope that even readers who shudder at that thought might find what is said here interesting, for surely the criticisms levelled at the Church by its socially concerned young members are not relevant to Catholicism alone. Although Catholicism will be my main point of religious departure, this is in no sense intended as an intramural book. Many activist Catholic students think of denominationalism as an anachronism, and what they think about religion, even when it appears in the form of criticism of the institutional church, is significant for all of Christianity and even for all religion.

A more obvious limitation upon this study is the narrowness of my own experience. I cannot demonstrate that these reflections might not have been better undertaken by someone further removed from the process. The overall view, statistical summation and criticism from the stance of age and experience are all being sacrificed here in exchange for a view from the eye of the storm—or at least from somewhere in its midst. I justify this sacrifice—and, indeed, the whole project—not by whatever importance these thoughts may have in terms of their objective truth but by the fact that a great many young people are thinking along the same lines. All the material that follows has the aim of making more understandable the rather conspicuous political and religious behavior of certain young people. To do this I will often engage in criticism of both church and state. I say this not so much to convince as to explain the convictions that we often act upon. If anyone *is* convinced, so much the better, but this is not a polemic even if it makes occasional use of polemical tone.

It is impossible to discuss the political and religious attitudes of today's students without first outlining some of the historical events and conditions which were crucial to their formation. The natural condition of the life of the young is change, and the process of change in which we are caught up is itself as important as the often passing values that it has produced. Isolated political and religious events are insignificant by themselves and only gain significance when they intersect the lives of people. This is especially true of young people, where the particular point of development at which such events intersect is crucial. With this in mind, I have simplified the presentation of this very complex subject as much as possible. The first chapter provides a painfully brief review of the events and conditions that have led to the formation of political and religious activism among students. Subsequent chapters deal in greater detail with issues and implications either raised by the first chapter or related to the process it describes. I hope that these fragments will, by the end of the book, have formed at least a rudimentary portrait in the reader's mind.

One final apologia: if anything I say is interesting enough to draw criticism, I suspect that the criticism will come first from my own friends who will feel that I have not been scathing enough in my criticism. All that I can say is that the book is not addressed primarily to them. If I offend the purity of some of our beliefs by presenting them in a form that the average reader, including the sympathetic but uninitiated adult, might understand, then I apologize in advance—but only slightly. I shall go on trying to talk to the people whose opinion may ultimately, for better or worse, determine the fate of our ideals.

"MOVE OVER"
students, politics, religion

1

a new generation

In drawing this sketch of the current student movement in terms of political and religious reform, I have relied heavily upon my own experience, because my education closely follows the time divisions I have chosen to use as a framework. I was in grammar school from 1950 to 1959, in high school from 1959 to 1963 and in college and law school until the date of this writing. I base this chapter on this coincidence because for me—and for many others, I believe—it is a significant one. The impact of events on a person largely depends upon the stage of his development at the time they occur. Obviously, this is especially true of the young.

Moreover, the span of my life as a whole corresponds to a period distinct enough to have earned for itself a number of distinguishing labels: the post-war era, the atomic age, the cold war period, the age of television, of cybernetics, of space travel, even the "post-Christian" and "post-modern" age. My generation was raised entirely in this revolutionary time without the roots in the pre-war period that older Americans share. This must be continually borne in mind if our development is to be understood. I was resting in my mother's womb through the last summer of the war, but did not show my face until the Bomb first fell and ushered in the new age. Even though others of my "generation" are older or younger than I, and their education may not necessarily follow the neat divisions that mine does, I think my immediate classmates and I can serve as a convenient model for this sketch of our growth.

The process described below is essentially that which has been undergone by most Catholic student "activists." I hope that their experience will form an adequate basis for generalization about religion and politics among students in general. I cannot presume that the forces which I found to deserve emphasis affected anyone besides myself in quite the same way. There are, of course, many ways in which my own experience might easily differ from that of others: my education was exclusively urban, for example, and exclusively in Catholic institutions until law school. Moreover, the rate of radicalization of different students varies widely, and I think that in many cases—among Catholic students, especially—it was slower than it was in mine. Then, too, religious considerations greatly increase the danger of such generalizing as I will do, since religious beliefs are difficult to describe or to compare. With these limitations in mind, this chronology is submitted as a broad biography of activists of my age. I hope that it will correspond in fact to the actual development of many activists. Subsequent chapters will explore in detail the issues which are raised here. Now they will be dealt with briefly as a means of placing them in the framework of our political and religious development.

THE COLD WAR

It is only in retrospect that I realize how deeply the atmosphere of the Cold War pervaded my early education. By the "Cold War" I mean not only the divisiveness between the Soviet Union and the United States, but a whole series of polarizations erected by church and state, in terms of which nearly all social values were presented to us. Catholic education, for reasons which we shall examine later on, exaggerated this kind of presentation, and this exaggeration was not confined to religion. Catholicism in general seemed to see all things in terms of a war between good and evil, and it was inevitable that the politics which we were taught in Catholic schools became shaped by this mentality.

The political aspect of this polarization is familiar enough. We were taught that the principal contenders in the world were the forces of Communism and democracy (sometimes called "freedom") and that virtually all international politics was based on the struggle between them. I was born a little late to appreciate the full flavor of McCarthyism, but the senator's influence was strong in the two parochial schools which I attended. I do not remember being distinctly afraid of a domestic Communist uprising; what is vivid in my mind is the way in which most recent history, and all international affairs, were made to serve the Cold War interpretation of reality.

This is not to pretend that, as grammar school children, we had a sense of anything like "international affairs;" but we did know a little history, and history was largely a story of conflict. Modern history was the story of a conflict that was all-embracing. Within this framework, no idea, no suggestion was neutral. Each was either a weakness or a weapon. Politics was anything but "the art of the possible." It was a game in which the stakes were survival itself. This approach did not encourage compromise or the exploration of middle ways between the clashing ideologies. Even criticism of our government was rendered a kind of heresy, unless it focused on the charge that the government was not fighting Communism hard enough—due, no doubt, to "subversion."

It would not surprise me to hear that children have always been taught in such polarized terms. Grammar school is hardly the place to develop a healthy capacity for self-criticism. The threat of atomic war, however, substantially affected what otherwise might have been a typical introduction to politics. The Bomb raised the stakes and underpinned the whole struggle with the threat of sudden defeat and death. Although this was true for adults as well as for children, some of the war-weary previous generation looked upon the Bomb as an instrument of peace, because it had seemed to end World War II. It could never seem so to us. We saw it—when we dared look at it closely—for what it was, an instrument of terror. This is not to say that we did not believe along with everyone else that terror might preserve peace, but we never thought of that peace as comfortable or permanently tolerable.

I think now that the Bomb must have had an enormous effect on the children whose whole lives were lived in its shadow. At the time we did not perceive the thoroughness of its influence. Most of us expected that Russia might attack at any moment, and this fear was nurtured, (if not created in the first place), by frequent, unscheduled air-raid drills. Many of these were city-wide, and when the sirens broke the silence of the classroom we had no way of knowing whether or not *this* time it was the real thing. I can evoke quite easily the memory of crouching huddled under our desks, wondering how the bomb might sound, shielding our faces from flying glass, musing indecisively about the mystery of fallout. Was this a part of the experience of the children of the 40's or of any previous generation? In any case, it is one reason why the revulsion at the bombing of North Vietnam felt by so many of my generation does not suprise me.

What were the effects of this education in fear, buttressed by the threat of death? The effect on our first idea of politics has already been described: politics was war, not a process of mutual adjustment with harmony as its object. We were simply at war with the forces of Communism, and the only reason the war was not "hot" was that neither side dared start what promised to be the last war of all—the Russians out of cowardice or duplicity, and our side because of our nobility. But war it was.

The other striking effect of this indoctrination was the formation of our first notions of warfare and violence in general. Fear of Communism bred enormous resentment among us, and this often turned to simple hatred. The feeling was strong that the defeat of Hitler should have brought peace to the world at last, and that only the greed of the Communists still kept the world in danger. I suspect that a great many of us would have been relieved if the United States had surprise-attacked the Russians and put an end to the tensions to which we had so unjustly been subjected. We became quite casual about the thought of destroying whole nations in minutes, and also rather too confident of the effectiveness of bombing—a delusion obviously not confined to my age group. Whether television violence was a cause or effect of this atmosphere is not really relevant, but it fitted neatly into a mood with which we had lived since birth.

An important characteristic of this new violence was its impersonality. Americans thought before that destruction should be unleashed only on palpably evil enemies, like marauding Indians or Nazi storm troopers. But my generation was bred on a different kind of violence: since in our wars entire populations are the target, we began to think in terms of whole peoples, not just their soldiers, being the "enemy." I stress this atmosphere of violence so heavily only to make more clear the reaction to it that followed.

None of this was a question of liberalism or conservatism. As far as we were concerned, there was just one American ideology, and it was equally the basis of conservative saber-rattling and liberal talk of containment. We heard neither the rattling nor the discourse. We considered ourselves as Democratic or Republican, because our parents were. But our party affiliation did not extend to issues or, at least, not to international ones. Even domestic politics reflected the habit of polarization. Were not the major parties engaged in a battle between business and labor, between rich man and poor man? All politics and most human affairs was a matter of good guys against bad guys.

Our religious training resembled our political indoctrination. Catholic doctrine, as we were taught it, lent itself to presentation in polarized terms. Morality was presented as a system of laws which, if broken, resulted in a loss of grace and possible damnation. The enemies of Catholicism, (Protestants, for example), were equated with Communists. I think that I was well into my adolescence before I began to realize that

Protestants were sincere and not consciously rebellious Catholics who were embarrassed to confess their error. Again, the emphasis was on individuals as members of a group or adherents of an ideology, and not as persons.

The resemblance went even farther than that, because the political and religious ideologies were mixed. For Catholics the struggle against Communism has always been seen in quasi-religious terms. Communism is depicted more as a form of atheism than as a political or economic structure. This was not merely a result of nationalism. Communism was considered Christianity's greatest enemy, and the fear of a "Communist victory" and a general persecution of religion—especially Catholicism—reached the level of obsession and sometimes, seemingly, of paranoia. At the same time, Catholics have been extraordinarily anxious to prove themselves patriotic ever since immigrant Catholics were attacked by a bigoted Protestant majority for their seemingly-divided loyalty to Church and state. This close identification of politics and religion was not a grammar-school phenomenon only. Even today an examination of a large portion of the Catholic press (New York's *Catholic News,* the Brooklyn *Tablet,* or the Los Angeles *Tidings,* for example) will reveal that news about Communism—not just about Communist-Catholic disputes— is a regular feature. This was the character of my early education in politics and religion: grammar school was a womb furnished in black and white.

In 1959 I left for high school, just another department of the same institution with more homework. I had grown, however, and had begun to discover my identity as an individual. After a short while divisions began to appear in the mass of identical students. Most went on accepting uncritically everything they were told but a few, so very few at first, began to strike out on their own. Somehow we caught a glimpse of color and became uneasy in the training-places of the color-blind.

Politically, there was nothing for our uneasiness to latch on to. The spirit—or lack of spirit—of the Eisenhower administration, under which we had lived for as long as we had been literate, had cast a pall over politics. The "silent generation" refused to offer inspiration to its younger brothers, and there was no political figure on the scene capable of generating interest, let alone excitement. We were not yet impatient, however, because we had always thought of politics as distant and uninteresting. Change was not sought or even desired, since change was not a possibility; and growing older did not seem to hold much political promise, since the country at large—meaning adult America—was suffering from the same malaise. Our one really political notion was a sense of frustration over the threat of destruction. The constant possibility of war began to lead some of us to think that the world was led by madmen (perhaps even some from our part of the world); but this was a situation over which we could not hope to exert control for years, if ever.

Religion was both better and worse off: better, because at the time it occupied a larger part of our time than politics did, and worse, because we were so utterly impotent in its grasp. For a long time laziness was the only real enemy of our Catholicism. Despite the hyperbolic warnings drummed in by grammar school teachers, the danger was oversleeping on a Sunday morning rather than doubting what we all more or less accepted as immutable truth. Although religion occupied more of our time—if not our thoughts—than politics, this does not mean that we found religion more interesting. It affected our lives more obviously, and in that sense it held more of our interest; but except for those who were thinking of entering the service of the church, religion was not a subject of real interest or discussion. There were no real religious *issues* save for some few fine points of theology to be haggled over after class.

The discovery of sex opened up the first seam in our religious consensus. Religion had opposed laziness, which was a vice which we found easy to despise, or at least to feel embarrassed about. But when religion seemed to oppose sex, this was a different story. It met head-on with an instinct and interest which was a good deal harder to shrug off. The theology involved, as well as the actual conflicts that occurred, are equally irrelevant. The point is that sex was powerful and close to us, and though most of us took religion's side when the two came into conflict, (or repented when we did not), the discovery of a real gulf between instinct and education left us uneasy.

In its earliest forms, of course, this conflict was nothing new. The body said "do", and the church said "don't," as most bodies and most churches always have. If anyone finds this shocking, I should point out that we were taught that to enjoy kissing was mortally sinful. The discovery of sex led to the usual number of "defections" from the Church and the usual amount of soul-searching on the part of those who remained. It was our first real soul-searching, and it should be distinguished from the kind of conflict occasioned by a later and more mature exploration of sexuality and Catholicism, which deserves a chapter of its own below. That conflict centered around *sexuality* . This one centered around *sex*.

So we entered the 60's not entirely satisfied with either our politics or religion but with no substitutes in sight. Then John Kennedy and Pope John XXIII entered our simple world and lent direction to our discontent.

THE BIRTH OF THE MOVEMENT: 1960-1963

The effect of these two men on youth was out of all proportion to their actual accomplishments. This will remain a paradox unless it is understood that it was not their achievements, but the symbolism of their spirit, that excited and inspired us. We entered the 60's on the threshold of adulthood, and they were the central figures in our first adult experience of politics and religion. That first experience was change. President Kennedy and Pope John presented us with political and religious styles focused on change and adaptation to new circumstances. Their effect was measured by our yearning for release from two traditions in which change seemed impossible, a yearning born of our growing older in institutions which seemed not to recognize us and fanned by the deliberate rhetoric of the president and the pope.

The campaign and election of John Kennedy was the political birth of my generation. This was the first election that we followed closely and the first in which we understood, and took sides on, the issues. Not all of this loyalty was on a very sophisticated level (I was 15, and a high school sophomore), but it was new and strong despite its naivete—as we were. Kennedy's victory, in our eyes, was a victory for youth. When he told us that the torch had been passed to a new generaton, we believed that he thought of us as part of it.

Moreover, Kennedy seemed to lift the mantle of death off the nation's shoulders. It was he who for the first time said (loudly enough so we could hear) that war with Communism was not only not inevitable, but a stupid and dangerous idea. Kennedy rarely used the terms "total victory" or "balance of terror" when he spoke about international affairs. We were almost blind to the reality of Vietnam and the Bay of Pigs, and especially of the brinkmanship of the Cuban missile crisis. The reality we perceived was the symbolic reality of the triumph of possibility embodied in the character of the Kennedy administration. Since hope is the chief earmark of the young, we seized upon the hope for radical change. We did not see then that very few changes were being made.

The Kennedy years signalled the dissolution of political consensus for my generation. Perhaps this would have occurred anyway. This is one of the many points in this analysis where we might wonder whether we changed our thinking because of events or simply because we matured. Perhaps our evolving discovery of our individuality and identity would have led to differentiation and an end of consensus whether or not a catalyst had appeared. The important fact is that activists—those whose attitudes and actions responded to changing circumstances—introduced conflict and, eventually, ideology into our bleak political conversation. The liberals among us began to cluster together and to seek ways of expressing our new-found faith. The conservatives, equally happy that a real debate had started, rallied to their own standard-bearers. The resulting discussion was our essential political education. More than any academic study or independent examination of the works of political thinkers, it was our thrashing out among ourselves, year after year, of the political, social and religious issues with which we were confronted that shaped our politics and our political behavior.

The reaction to Pope John was more gradual. He had been pope for two years before the election of 1960; but it was the Second Vatican Council—again, its impact as much as, or more than, its actions—which left his mark upon the church and upon us. From the beginning, he had our sympathy, if only because his public personality compared favorably with that of his predecessor and with our notion of what we could expect a pope to be. Although he won favor in certain circles of the church and among many outside the Catholic Church, it was his later encyclicals and the Council which prompted a large part of the revolution in religion that has engulfed this phase of our religious consciousness. Again, the effect out-weighed the cause. Pope John opened new avenues, but they have been extended by others much further than he probably intended.

The Second Vatican Council, by its very existence more than by any of its pronouncements, served a function much like President Kennedy's in bringing to an end the myth of consensus. What we witnessed in the Council was the spectacle of a radically divided church. Although the spirit of the Council was remarkable in its unity and sometimes forced unanimity, and also demonstrated in many ways the church's strength and cohesiveness, Vatican II revealed to many Cath-olics how deeply divided the Church is on many major issues. We had been taught that the church was the guardian of ab-solute religious truth somehow always at its disposal. Certain doctrines were undefined merely because the requisite inspira-tion had not materialized. Sooner or later each difference of opinion would be resolved, probably by papal pronounce-ment.

The fact and character of the debate in the Council altered our whole notion of the means by which religious truth was to be discovered. As students we perceived the crucial impor-tance of bringing all kinds of learning to bear on the solution of "religious" problems; there emerged a new premium on study, and many of us became seriously interested in the study of theology in particular. (Ironically, at the time it was impos-sible for lay students to specialize in theology at most Catholic universities.) We also discovered the existence of factions within the church and dimly perceived the part we might play in them. For the very first time it seemed that we might eventually be able to exert some influence on the formulation of Church policy and doctrine as laymen, and not as clergymen.

This is especially worth noting because it parallels what was happening in the political area. As I mentioned earlier, we always felt powerless. This weakness was particularly acute in our relation to the church. While we hoped that some day we might have political power, if only through the feeble voice of the ballot, power in the religious institution lay forever out of our grasp. It was the exclusive domain of priests. Now we saw that change was possible in the church, and that we might eventually influence its direction. This revelation caused a far-reaching restructuring of the relationship of the church to many of her most concerned and articulate young members.

Pope John influenced us more directly through his encyclicals, which we will discuss later. His inspiration was only the starting point of a larger process. His writings on social issues succeeded in tying the processes of political and social change together in my generation's consciousness. We have just seen that political and religious change was seized upon by young people uneasy with the powerlessness of youth. It becomes clear that these two processes are really aspects of the adaptation of the young to institutions that structure much of their social behavior. The principal thrust of all the change spoken of thus far has been toward the enhancement of the person and the dilution of the institution's power to manipulate him. This will be the theme of many of these reflections.

My viewpoint is that the flux of the early 60's unified the political and religious consciousness of the activist Christian

student. Religion and politics had already been partially identi-
fied by the institutions themselves: witness the church's attitude towards Communism and vice-versa. But our identification of the two was not the old confusion of the debate about
whether or not we should get political lectures from the pulpit;
rather, it derived from our increasing inability to keep separate our various standards of criticism. The church was subjected to "political" criticisms—for her totalitarianism, for
example—and the government was attacked on the grounds
of morality. This was not so much a question of confusion as it
was of unification. Raised in a world in which inexorable
political machines threatened our lives, where our church
taught that a war between good and evil threatened our souls,
we developed a unified ideal, however unconscious at first,
which sought to answer the flaws in both institutions. That
ideal was an image of the person, unobjectified, and un-
manipulated; and it found its active expression in what we
usually call the "movement," the loosely knit but cohesive
body of student activists which is the defined arena of this
study.

These are the origins of the movement. There remains only
to describe its progress and to place in broad perspective its
more specific aspects. This chronology will be largely a political one since the religious aspect of the movement has been
less dependent upon events. Involvement with religious
change led to the formation of cells of students, lay people and
clergy which were more or less underground, depending upon
their own radicalism, and the attitude of the local church
authorities. We will discuss this development of religious
groups in more detail later on. For now, we will only date the
formation of most of these groups in late 1964 and say that
they continue to arise in new forms and new locations.

The first great experience of political activity for my generation was the civil rights movement. This had been started earlier on a much smaller scale by black people and a relatively few white adults and students. It was our training ground, and we developed a good many of our tactics there, especially the art of demonstrating. Moreover, for Christian students the civil rights movement increased their identification of political and religious values, and the struggle developed a strong moral overtone that was eventually carried over into other areas of politics. Its overall significance for our study lies in the fact that it was the first student movement in American history of any significant proportions, and its occasional successes gave us our first experience of political power and our introduction to the mechanics of social change.

THE RADICALIZATION OF THE MOVEMENT: 1963-1969

Even before the deaths of Pope John and President Kennedy, the movement began to grow beyond their inspiration toward insight born of our first involvement in the new life of political and religious activity. Both men were, after all, essentially *conservative* even in their attempts at reform; and it was not long before we began to hope that not only would the change they called for come about, but that change would accelerate and affect our political and religious institutions more basically. The era of liberal reform had been a breath of fresh air for us after the stifling simple-mindedness of our early education; but once we got into the habit of breathing, we began to notice more and more how much of the atmosphere remained foul. Disappointment with the failure of the Council to deliver on its promise of renewal and with President Kennedy's halting legislative progress led to an increase in activity

and a decline in confidence in the president and the pope and
in authority figures in general.

Then things took a turn for the worse. Both men died. They
were replaced with men far more cautious in reform than they
had been. Pope Paul and President Johnson took office with
the support of most members of the movement; both soon lost
it. This was due partly to their own conservatism although
President Johnson accomplished far more than President
Kennedy had. But the main reason why both pope and president lost support was that students extended their predecessors' premises further and further beyond the dimensions of
the change that was actually taking place.

In the early 60's I remember having no strong identification
with a "generation." When President Kennedy spoke of a
"new generation" he meant everyone under 50 (if he meant
anyone at all), and we were content to identify ourselves with
that larger group. I started college in 1963, and I found that
group identification was much stronger on campus than it was
off campus. Moreover, our continual discussion of political
and religious issues led to a refinement of our viewpoints and
to the establishment of an increasingly extensive body of
shared opinion. The civil rights movement continued the
process. It brought together students from different parts of
the country, exposed Catholic students to Protestant and non-
religious activists and generally laid the groundwork for the
mass organizations of the New Left.

A major cause of the radicalization of the movement was
disappointment with the accomplishments, and finally with
many of the premises, of conventional liberalism. The civil
rights movement failed despite the passage of sweeping legislation, because the roots of racism in America are deeper than
the jurisdiction of our courts. The steady escalation of the war

in Vietnam in the mid-60's led to a large-scale abandonment of the civil rights movement by students, who flung their energy into the rapidly growing and more fundamentalist peace movement. This made the rise of black power militancy more possible, because it returned decisive control of the activist civil rights organizations to blacks.

This massive shift in the focus of student political activity showed clearly that treating just one issue at a time confined the energies of the movement, that the causes of militarism and racism were deep, and that their cure depended on more radical measures than a new law or an end to one war. Out of this double realization the New Left was born as the *organizational expression of the unified social consciousness of the student activist elite*. The New Left, principally exemplified by the Students for a Democratic Society (SDS), calls for a reform of our society to end manipulation of persons by institutions either by racial oppression at home or by economic exploitation and military aggression abroad. Despite its largely secular character, the personalist element of the New Left closely resembles the theologically-oriented personalism of Christian student activists. Many of the latter have associated themselves with the New Left.

The continued radicalization of the New Left does not concern us here, except as an indication of one of the directions that change is taking. The period from 1963 to 1967 was one of increasing despair and increasing militancy, as riots swept ghettos every summer, and the war continued to escalate in the face of growing opposition. In early 1968 a great many students had despaired of the efficacy of the democratic process altogether, as it is presently structured in this country. The Eugene McCarthy and Robert Kennedy campaigns raised new interest and hope in the possibility of change through

direct political action; but the death of Senator Kennedy, and
the failure of Senator McCarthy to secure the Democratic
nomination for President, may yet prove to have destroyed all
faith in the American political system among a significant portion of the nation's students.

In the next few chapters this whole process will be examined again, and an attempt will be made to separate the
threads of education, politics and religion from the tangled
mass of events that formed our thinking.

2

the classroom crisis

Although student activists have been most prominent in university reform, the meaning of their protest has been misunderstood in the universities more often than in any other place. To place student views on education in context it is necessary to consider what their experience of education has been. In this chapter I will describe and criticize my own Catholic education in some detail, and I will try to draw on that description to explain some of the major objections of students to the manner in which they are being educated. Using the Catholic system as a model has several advantages. I know it best; it will provide necessary background for the discussion of religion itself later, and it will help in our consideration of American educational problems in general. Students believe that the central problems in American education derive from its sectarianism. This means that university education (and, analogously, all schooling) is designed to perpetuate a particular culture which supports it. A close examination of Catholic education—where the sectarian features are very explicit—will serve as a good introduction to a broader discussion of the subject.

Young Catholics usually rebel against their religion first in terms of their religious education. For American Catholics, whose church has laid such stress on its educational system, religion is more an in-school than an in-church experience until college. Whether a controversial religious issue was theological, institutional, liturgical or a matter of the church's "social" teaching, the arena for the argument was the classroom and the campus. Moreover, for many years most Catholic children's only contact with the clergy is at school or at instruction classes. We rarely spoke to priests in our parishes and the priests at school were the only members of the clergy who knew us as individuals. Our dialogue with the official Church at least consisted mainly in this contact. To understand the relation of young people to the Church, it is necessary to understand their religious education. This is why it makes such an excellent model for the whole educational question.

Perhaps the oppressiveness of grammar school for me was the result of peculiar circumstances. I spent the first four years and some months of my education at a large parochial school on New York's West Side, and to the best of my recollection I found it a very pleasant place, to the extent that school could be pleasant for a small boy in the midst of the city's distractions. The school enrolled both boys and girls, but the sexes virtually never saw each other, since they not only used separate classrooms, but separate entrances to the building. During the first four years we were taught by nuns, or by elderly laywomen, but when we entered the fifth grade we were old enough to be educated by men (being on the brink of manhood ourselves). In this case the men were Christian Brothers, members of a religious community founded in 18th Century France and dedicated exclusively to the education of boys—the girls stayed on with the laywomen and the nuns.

Just two months into my fifth grade we moved to a new neighborhood, and I transferred to a very old and tiny school staffed entirely by nuns, where boys and girls shared the same classrooms. There were a great many things wrong with that school, and in retrospect it is not easy to sort them out into the relevant and the incidental. The aspect that stands out most clearly has already been mentioned—the emphasis on polarities rather than unities. Of course, this was very early education and many things do need to be presented in that way. But I think it would have been better for some of us had people not been explained away and generalized out of consideration. We had a very strong identification as Catholics, and we had from the start a feeling that it was us against everyone else— not just the godless—but everyone who was not Catholic. In my case I cannot imagine that this had much effect since we lived in one of the most heterogenous sections of New York and came constantly face to face with people who were different from us; but it must have imbued in many a real fear of the different and a chauvinism that would later transform itself quite naturally into bigotry.

One thing that those years impressed upon me was that nuns should never teach boys. The teachers in my school, being female, had female attitudes toward achievement; the greatest award they could conceive of, for example, was to openly praise students who did well. The girls would blush with pride when their accomplishments were drawn in detail for the admiration of the class; but a boy would squirm and seethe in the same situation: doing well was a girl's game, and he wanted none of it—he was embarrassed in front of the other boys. This had not always been so; in the all-boy classes of my first school there was competition even among the seven- and eight-year-olds. School was a contest, and we took pride in getting stars in our books, and all the other paramilitary paraphernalia attached to success. But no one wanted to be teacher's pet when the teacher was a nun who would nearly call you that out loud, and think it a compliment.

It was bad enough being a boy there; it was worse being in any way an unusual one. The teachers were not prepared to cope with anyone who was different, and the tight-knit structure of the classroom provided no outlet for ideas that could not be enjoyed in common. Those who were more stupid or more bright than the others were pretty much cut off from the group. Although they soon enough discovered that they were not like everyone else, the system did not include a means of discovering why. I never got into the rhythm of the place. After a while I lost interest, went as infrequently as I dared and was accused of dullness and truancy. After a while, I began to believe it. When it came time to apply to high schools, I set my sights on a large, middle-range school where I was sure I could fit in. When we arrived they put us through several days of testing and placed me in the "honors" class, and literally saved my academic life. Several of the grammar school honors students came to high school with me. They were the meek, pliant, plodding boys, and in a large and competitive all-boys high school they quickly settled near the bottom of the heap. The nuns must have been doing *something* wrong.

There is no point in merely dragging out for one more hiss all the evils of learning by rote. As I see it, rote learning was simply a natural pedagogical adaptation to the idea that the "truth of Catholicism" was embodied in a system of formulas. All learning in grammar school was by rote, and all subjects were rendered difficult and dull by this method of learning. I am sure geography bored me more than religion did. Religion, at least, held out a promise of mystery. Grammar school teachers were concerned not with the formation of critical minds but with placing at our disposal enough facts to evaluate later on. After all, Mary Perkins Ryan had not yet raised the question in her excellent tract, *Are Parochial Schools The Answer?*

Moreover, an adult examination of a catechism may not reveal how the same book will strike a child. To those young enough still to have some senses unblunted, even the catechism contained an element of wonder. Nor is it fair to say that religion as taught in grammar school was irrelevant; it was the one thing that was supremely relevant. I disliked geography (and later, algebra) because at the time they seemed in no way connected to my life. But "Why did God make me?" was a momentous question, even if the answer was taken for granted. This is not to say that religion in grammar school was not far removed from adult reality. It merely stresses that it was central to a child's reality.

This was precisely what was so terribly wrong with it. Religion was not a preparation for adulthood in the way that our other subjects were because it did not lend itself to growth but only to expansion. As we grew older the religion we were taught grew more and more complicated and detailed, but the change was merely structural and quantitative. We saw religion as a collection of facts and faith as belief in their factuality despite or because of their implausibility. Learning by

rote was suited to the other subjects because we ultimately did
not have to have faith in them. We could un-learn them all
later without disillusionment if we had to. Religion, on the
other hand, was incorporated into our lives. To have to discard the religious simplicity of our childhood was to grow
older consciously, and the jettisoning of religious naivete was
not accomplished without a certain loss of faith.

This takes for granted that religion was taught humanely,
and that what was taught was not itself objectionable. Grammar school religion was not the continuing horror story that
some claim it was. If I am not merely forgetting the un-
pleasant, it seems to me that it was too optimistic. I have
friends, especially girls, who claim that religion was presented
in terms so laden with fear and sin that later rebellion against
it was like liberation from slaveɪy. This attitude is particularly
common among those who studied at all-girls Catholic high
schools where apparently the problem of sex comes to
dominate religious teaching completely to a truly morbid degree. That was not the case in any of the schools that I attended. Religion was concerned with the war between good
and evil, but it seems to me that good always had the upper
hand. Confession occurred at more frequent intervals than our
"sins" did, and most of us had to tax our imaginations to
compile a list of things to confess.

The nuns in my school were frightening not because they
gave fire and brimstone sermons. These would have been fun.
We each secretly knew that only the boy in the *next* seat
would go to hell. They frightened me, at least, because they
were often harsh and unsympathetic and sometimes cruel.
Physical punishment was common. Hardly a day passed without some instance of it. When we saw the "trouble-makers" of
the class slapped, we probably felt more self-righteous than

afraid; but often there were beatings for not having had the right answer, or for having failed to complete an assignment. These were not the more genteel spankings of the early days of high school when we leaned against the blackboard hoping that the teacher would not notice that we had stuffed our back pockets to dull the blows. In grade school punishment was not a ritual but a fit of temper. I once saw a nun slap a girl's face so hard that her nose gushed blood all over the notebook she had raised to protect herself.

I suppose I am confessing here how much I hated them, or most of them, at least; but if "hate" seems too strong a word I should add that I also hated girls, school sweaters, and lining up after lunch. I despised the female formalism of the place with all the contempt that a boy could muster at the thought of being paraded by women. No one should mistake the regimentation of a grammar school run by nuns with the discipline of a military academy, as the nuns were wont to do. In the latter, one submits to control in order to develop one's sense of discipline; in the former, one is subjected to control in order to gratify someone's sense of orderliness. I hated the whole business because it wounded my sensitive, pre-adolescent pride; but I hated the nuns more intensely because they succeeded in making me afraid of them. It was my first bitter lesson in the gulf between the practice and preaching of Christianity.

The transition from grammar school religion as taught and practiced by nuns to high school religion as taught by priests was a process of careful debunking: it was an attempt to administer disillusionment in large enough doses to produce immunity but small enough to prevent despair. Many of the boys who started high school with me were from nuns' schools, and for us the contrast was exhilarating. Everything about high school seemed masculine: even prayers before class were said in a new, lower key. The coming on of puberty and the beginnings of some kind of intelligence had eroded our faith towards the end of grammar school and made us embarrassed by a religion we found tailor-made for girls. The priests in early high school made it their job to combat this common sentiment by dressing up religion in the garb of apologetics. The effect of this was merely to develop in us a facility to find rational reasons for our narrowness of mind, but at first it served an important function in our liberation from the religious education of our childhood.

If the cornerstone of grammar school religion was memorization, the same place was filled in high school by method. In the first year we studied our first science, and our first algebra; and we studied Latin, not so much as a language as a linguistic method. It was natural enough, then, that method should have been applied to the teaching of religion. "Faith" was still a matter of facts and formulas, but now these were shown to flow logically from one another rather than to appear as a single, full-blown revelation. The process was one of masculinization. Before this time, religion was geared for emotional stimulation; now the aim was intellectual challenge and satisfaction. It worked well at first. Our teachers had the advantage of our complete cooperation and enthusiasm, and some won our special loyalty by openly making fun of the nuns. We had already been taught to regard ourselves as a beleaguered minority. Now our teachers emphasized that this should not upset us because we also enjoyed the distinction of being absolutely right.

Two forces eventually began to assert themselves against this spiritualized smugness. One was sexual, the elemental revolt against the imposition of mental categories on the sensual and the instinctive. I cannot believe that many of us sur-

vived high school without in some way violating the rigid
sexual standards provided in the classroom, since they were so
rigid that the most ordinary conduct was prohibited. The
sexual ethic was a simple rule-of-thumb: sex could not be
enjoyed physically before marriage. Now it was not possible
for us to date for any length of time without ending up kissing
someone seriously, that is, in any other way than we would on
her doorstep, with her father looking on. Yet though this kind
of behavior was demanded of us socially, we were taught that
if we caught ourselves *liking* it we would damn our souls to
hell forever. In lapsing from this kind of impossible standard
we had to ask whether we believed that result would really
follow, and the ways in which we answered that question
established our broader attitudes toward orthodoxy.

The second force that worked against our custom-made
consensus was the increasing self-awareness and self-confi-
dence that some sixteen- and seventeen-year-olds developed as
they set out on their own intellectually. Up until this point
they could not be distinguished from one another on an intellectual basis since few students had ideas of their own. In the
last years of high school, however, some of the better students
went on a binge of self-education and for the first time began
to discuss the different things they had read on their own. This
substantially changed the atmosphere of the classrooms: while
before we either asked questions or talked about some point
made by the teacher, now some students brought ideas from
the outside into the discussion. Our earlier acquaintance with
"non-Catholic" ideas had been through our teachers, who
would outline them to us before refuting them. Now students
were objecting to some of the teachers' contentions; but when
the teachers had not framed the objections, their refutations
were often less convincing. Intellectual doubt made its first

appearance, and the teachers were unable to dispel it. Since they were often harsh with the students who disagreed with them, some stopped trying to win their point and quietly disbelieved what they were taught.

Those who disagreed formed the beginnings of what we later called the activist group of students. They were, of course, a distinct minority. Many Americans seem to find a curious satisfaction in this fact: every once in a while it will be pointed out in the press that the rowdy students who are doing all the protesting are only a tiny minority, and one might imagine that sighs of relief can be heard in living rooms all across the country. Rejection of what was taught, with a consequent loss of teachers' approval, was not something that many students dared. Again, some Americans seem to believe that only a naturally rebellious student would want to. But it was the better students who disagreed; the mediocre ones accepted everything they were told. Not every good student became an activist, but far fewer poor ones did. Most of what is said hereafter about students refers to the leaders of the student population and not to their followers or to followers of any kind.

Certainly the atmosphere of my high school did not encourage this kind of dissent. My experience may have been atypical, since I was in an honors section through all four years and was therefore effectively insulated from the school at large; but my twin brother went through the same school at the same time, and our impressions remain identical. My teachers, who were in most cases the heads of the academic departments, were generally conservative or middle-of-the-road, but they were also tolerant of disagreement and, at least politically, impartial in class. Almost all the other teachers in the school were very conservative, and it was a common source of humor that they were so open in their attempts to convert their classes to their way of political thinking. One teacher opened his class on the morning after Eleanor Roosevelt died with "Happily, one more Red is dead." The class indicated enthusiastic assent. When I accuse the faculty and students of conservatism, I do not mean a more than usually rigid adherence to tradition or a reluctance to accept radical change. I mean undisguisedly anti-intellectual and rabid anti-Communism plus religious and political chauvinism approaching pure bigotry.

That most students shared these sentiments is not surprising. They were mostly lower-middle-class Irish- and Italian-Americans, and their thinking followed the clearly discernible pattern of their parents' voting. However, it is not this mass, but those who withdrew from it, who are our concern. These latter were the "liberals," the ones who had been attracted by John Kennedy, who found increasingly that there was not enough food for their liberalism at school, and who therefore undertook to educate themselves. It is almost a cliché among college students that they did more reading in their last year of high school than in any year since. This was more than usually so at Catholic schools where whole worlds of experience were excluded from class and where the distinguishing characteristic of liberal as opposed to conservative students was their degree of curiosity. To become interested in subjects outside the curriculum was to become committed to independent study, and independent study almost invariably led to dissatisfaction and eventual revolt.

The greatest fans of our early introduction to apologetics were the budding intellectuals. They were reacting against the simplistic emotionalism of grammar school religion. Towards the end of high school the intellectual group split into two factions: the larger liberal group began to revolt against the apologetic method after it had led them to new kinds of thinking which often shook their faith; a smaller conservative group continued to try to assimilate all new insights in the framework of their very traditional faith, often with great success. They formed the bulk of the "intellectual Right" on campus, the followers of William F. Buckley, Jr. The rabid anti-intellectual mass does not merit much more discussion, especially since they did not become a significant segment of the campus population. Only Catholic colleges would take them. The more relevant battle later on would be between the activist and the apathetic in a mass of students who are almost all at least ostensibly liberal.

This factionalization was not limited to Catholic schools although I might have made it seem too dependent upon the unique circumstances of religiously sectarian education. All American education is sectarian. The prep student in New England is caught in a system as rigid as the Catholic system. Sectarian education traps the student in a mid-western public high school and the bright Jewish student in a New York special high school. Each has one hope: to attempt to educate himself in spite of demands for strict conventionalism, sterilized education for the middle class or anti-valuative relativism. The least sectarian of our schools are in inner-city ghettos, simply because so few teachers there feel that they are preparing their students to take their places. Our ghetto communities are the only American communities which do not in effect maintain their own school systems; everywhere else, educational institutions exist to perpetuate and recruit for the culture that created them. In most schools, then, there develops a splitting off into those who accept that culture passively, those who accept it fervently and become its apologists, and those who seek its transformation or destruction. Close examination of the course of students within the Catholic system is especially valuable because the Catholic tradition is explicit, while the other systems, lacking a "siege mentality," hide their cultural shackles behind a veil of shared assumptions.

Because the Catholic tradition was more explicit its limitations were more open to attack. The main thrust of the criticism was aimed at the anti-liberalism of the way in which we were educated. We had thought of Christianity as a unifying force that could make cohesive different approaches to the study of man; but the more we studied, the more we discovered was excluded. Catholic dogma, dependent as it was upon Greek and Medieval philosophy, held up an image of man that the rest of the world had rejected since at least the last century. Oriental philosophy, psychoanalysis, the theater of the absurd, technology, existentialism—all seemed difficult to reconcile with what we had been taught about the stability and clarity of things. We regarded certainty as the earmark of our religion and were thus cut off from whole areas of knowledge where uncertainty was accepted or even enshrined. I read a passage somewhere in Emerson once which suggested that the man who was really loyal to truth would always hover *between* certainties; its relativism made me furious. I felt the same reaction to a section of Albert Schweitzer's autobiography in which he discussed his early theological thinking on the problem of Christ's self-awareness of his divinity: it seemed to me a cowardly refusal to either affirm or deny Christ's divinity by ignoring the objective and dwelling on the subjective. Now that speculation of both kinds comes quite naturally to me, I shudder at my early intolerance.

We were being educated in the nineteenth century. We

were not supposed to feel or even notice the profound uneasiness of our own age, except to write it off as proof of the disastrous effects of unbelief. The "death of God" was *the* religious problem of the decade, but we had no idea what it was really about. The smug references to atheism we heard in class told us nothing of man's confrontation with the absurd or of the efforts of existentialists and others to discover a way for him to survive it. That struggle was the basis of most of the literature of this century, and our outside reading brought us suddenly into contact with a whole world that challenged the reality of our own. Either the conscience of modern man was asking the wrong questions or else our tradition had too complacently satisfied itself with the wrong answers. Since we had been taught that faith was belief, our faith was shaken.

Of course we were not the only ones in the world who were untouched by the crisis of unbelief, or, indeed, by any of the crises of our age. It is my impression that only a very small number of people live "in" the present century. In some ways this is obvious: whole areas and peoples in India, Africa and Asia live no differently than their ancestors of a thousand years ago; and how many pockets of the 16th Century are left in Spain, of the 18th in Ireland, of the 19th everywhere? How many lives have actually been shaped by the revolutions of the last century in economics, technology and psychology? It seems that the distinctive characteristics of an age are merely the characteristics of its most obvious (often its most literate) groups while the life of everyone else is being changed only very slowly. Whether this be so or not, it startled students who gradually realized that their education had carefully separated them from the intellectual ferment of the era they were to control. In the division of loyalties that followed, tradition was sure to suffer among the most academically advanced and curious students. For some this meant simply that religion was abandoned, either as too heavy a burden, or as a deception to be rejected in bitterness; for others, it meant that the heart of Christianity must be separated from the traditions that encumber it, so that it might provide light amid modern relativism and despair.

Many of the latter went to Catholic colleges, spurred by the promises of the Vatican Council and the hope of the liberalization of Catholic campuses. Many could just as easily have gone to prominent secular colleges but felt that the humanistic atmosphere of the Catholic campus might be more conducive to the study of man as person rather than as a mechanism or pawn of his environment. This hope was frustrated in more cases than not because most Catholic colleges are mediocre.* Even when they are not mediocre, some of the negative aspects of Catholic traditionalism still hold sway. Catholic higher education is in the midst of so revolutionary a period that the Catholic university cannot properly be discussed except in terms of which directions it will follow as it changes.

I spent my undergraduate days at Fordham, a university which in five years has demonstrated everything that can be wrong with Catholic higher education, and many of the measures that may redeem it. It is unfortunate to have to divide the religious and academic problems of the university, especially since they have often been closely related; but it is at the same time impossible to discuss the paradox of Catholic higher education without looking carefully at the element that makes it paradoxical, that is, the place of theology in the curriculum and the relation of dogma to what is taught in all departments.

* For a damning assessment of Catholic graduate education, see Allan M. Cartter, *An Assessment of Quality in American Education,* (Washington, D.C.: American Council on Education, 1966), pp. 20-77.

In a larger sense what must be explained are some of the forces that changed Fordham from a university where the administration was paternalistic and authoritarian—as evidenced by its rules for student conduct—and where religious education was mediocre, to one in which the students are largely self-governing, and where there is at last quality in the theology curriculum.

Fordham, like most church-related colleges, used to pride itself on its requirement that all Catholic students take a heavy load of theology and philosophy courses. These requirements had been formulated at a time when secular colleges were dropping undergraduate courses in religion and theology and cutting back on their previous strong emphasis on philosophy. But because these courses were required, and because not many were excited by the prospect of teaching or taking them, they degenerated into a small group of survey courses that students and teachers suffered through. The teachers lectured with the same set of notes year after year, possibly generation after generation. When I arrived at Fordham there were just four theology courses and even fewer in philosophy. At the same time, however, secular universities were responding to increasing student interest in theology and philosophy. Most had a heavy philosophy curriculum—if somewhat lopsided in favor of Anglo-American philosophy—and a good many had substantial courses in religion. The church-related university, the self-proclaimed guardian of religious and philosophic values, allowed the level of its teaching to drop to that of a glorified high school curriculum and left serious theology to the seminaries and to secular Departments of Religion. As a sophomore I informed the Dean that I wished to major in theology and was told that there were not enough courses to form a major. In a leading Catholic university one could not make religion one's special branch of study!

This situation has changed and had already changed radically by the time I graduated. Today Fordham has a wide variety of undergraduate electives in theology, many of them not related directly to Catholicism and all of them supposedly taught impartially, without constant reference to dogma. The Department of Theology in the graduate school promises to be an outstanding source of both lay and clerical theologians in the future. This development directly contradicts the fear of those who believed that only continued educational conservatism on the part of church-related universities could preserve a strong faith among the educated members of the Church. On the contrary, during the years that a conservative policy held sway, theology aroused little interest on campus, and the courses were thought of as necessary evils for the attainment of a degree. Today, among those students from whom all interest in religion has not been driven by previous Catholic education, there is an unprecedented theological concern that can be linked directly to the openness and quality of the theological study provided by the university.

What is the significance of this development for Catholic higher education? It means the death of the anti-liberal principle that the best way to preserve the faith of students is to protect them from alien theologies and philosophies; it signals the end of the siege mentality so prevalent even among educated Catholics and so responsible for the traditional narrowness of Catholic education; and it generates a new respect for quality of thought, since the knowledgeable and intelligent student will now at last be considered more than the equal of the one who accepts what he is told without question and willingly parrots his teachers' thinking on exams. Liberal theology curricula will have an immeasurably strong ecumenical effect, since study leads to the perception of the common nature of today's religious problems and a concentration on interdenominational efforts toward their solution. Ultimately, the sharing of theological information and expertise with large numbers of students and laymen must lead to more humane procedures to be followed in the formulation of Church doctrine and policy.

Whether any of this affects the spirituality of the average student is a difficult question. Catholic universities used to be content if students went through the motions. Male students are usually not exceptionally devout. The most the school might hope for was that the student would absorb a certain amount of information about the church and that he would raise his children as Catholics. Still, the level of religious fervor among Catholic students must have been a continuing source of discouragement. The fact that theology has now become interesting to a larger number of students has not basically altered this situation. The number of students at Fordham during my time who would admit openly that they had no loyalty to the church was large by any standard; moreover, this group seemed to include a majority of the best students. The exceptions were bright conservative students and those with a special interest in theology or religion.

A good many of those who "defected" did so when they were in high school but came to Fordham to hide the fact from their parents, or because they found Fordham academically attractive. A smaller number found the contrast between high school and college religious attitudes unsettling and abandoned ship. Other casualties were those who studied theology seriously and rejected merely the denominationalism of the Church. A larger number were moved to doubt their very theism by exposure to radical theology. The revolution in attitudes towards the *teaching* of theology seems not to have had a significant effect on the practice of religion by these students. It has had other effects, however, and perhaps the distinction between "practicing" and "non-practicing" Catholic students is not the most important distinction that can be made in discussing the effects of such a change.

It should be noted that this change in curriculum came about in large part through pressure exerted by students. The drive towards a revised curriculum was only one part of a broad attack by students upon paternalistic administration of the university. At Fordham the effects were highly visible. In the span of a few years student government was transformed from a not very necessary supervisor of club activities to the bargaining agent for the student body. Assertion of student independence resulted in revisions in the norms for student conduct and a system whereby the norms were largely enforced by the students themselves. Whether students must wear ties in class is of little significance, but the way in which the university resolves such questions has far-reaching implications for the allocation of power within the university community. Many of the battles of the last few years at Fordham would have seemed anachronistic to students at secular colleges where administrations have been more consistently liberal. Nevertheless, Fordham has gone farther in her reforms than many a secular university, and the success of any such attempt at student-administration rapport is an aid to similar attempts elsewhere.

Even Fordham's attempts to update its "Catholicity" are significant for higher education in general. All education, again, is sectarian and a slave to the culture that maintains it. If Catholic education was for more than a century—and in most places still is—enslaved by a conservative religious tradition, secular higher education is also enslaved by both Americanism and a concept of liberalism that prevents administrators from making certain moral choices about the function of their universities. The fight to win places on Catholic theology faculties for non-Catholic theologians is not much different from the fight to win places on state university history faculties for Socialists or Communists. Attempts by Catholic students to force a re-evaluation of goals upon their universities, in terms of education instead of the preservation of the church, are no different from attempts by students to force re-definitions by secular universities in similar educational terms, instead of in terms of the preservation of the present structure of American society.

These student movements are not identical. In a sense they are directionally opposite. Catholic student activists want their universities to move from an excessive sense of morality towards greater liberalism, while many students at secular colleges want them to move from what they consider excessive liberalism towards a greater moral sensibility. The two groups are not working against each other but toward a common middle ground; and this is a phenomenon we shall encounter again and again if we examine the whole range of student activism. The efforts of the Catholic students will gain sympathy from most Americans more readily than the efforts of the others will because the American public is suspicious of explicit "indoctrination" but regards the political "impartiality" of universities as an important value.

The latter issue can be clearly framed by taking the example of the current student agitation against university involvement with military research. University administrators claim that they follow an impartial policy by permitting, say, the use of university faculty and facilities for research in chemical and biological warfare. Any faculty member or graduate student who disapproves of such research need not participate; those who do approve should be allowed to pursue any form of research they choose. Administrators say that for the university to prohibit certain kinds of research would be the same as forbidding the teaching of pacifism, or socialism. The university, in its benevolent liberalism, chooses not to take sides. These arguments undoubtedly have a strong effect on public opinion, if we can judge by the tone of editorials on student protests.

The question is not so simple. A call to the university not to contract with the government for the production of weaponry is not the same as a call for the dismissal of all professors who support the war. Presumably, the university would not contract with peace organizations to produce anti-government propaganda nor would it produce weapons for a foreign government. Students can well claim that real impartiality demands that the university not work for the government at all, except in demonstrably non-military areas, unless it will perform the same services for anyone who will pay for them.

This question of university involvement in military projects is only a single aspect of the current turmoil between activist students and university administrators. It is the kind of dispute that is fought out in public, and so it attracts wide attention. The quasi-political battles too often attract *all* the attention, so that student demands for *educational* reform are unnoticed or not understood by the public at large. This is unfortunate because the CIA-and-the-university sort of affair is merely a striking symptom of a more pervasive illness. There would be no issue at all were it not for the fact that a number of highly vocal students happen to oppose a particular war which universities have sometimes found it profitable to promote. This is not to say that the student criticism is not valid or that it should be discontinued; but such ostensibly partisan criticism should not be allowed to obscure the deeper issues which confront higher education, nor to draw off the energies of students who might otherwise find themselves in the forefront of the movement for broad reform.

What are those issues? They all relate to the universities' sectarianism and to the fact that our educational institutions are designed to prepare this generation to take the last generation's place. Education always involves a tenuous balancing of society's simultaneous commitments to its preservation and its reformation. Especially at universities, it has been at least tacitly admitted that society can survive only through frequent reaffirmations of its basic values and equally frequent reforms in its structure and in those of its values that have gone sour. Even a conservative might agree with John Henry Newman that "to live is to change," though he might not admit that "to be perfect is to change often." But it is not enough to admit that this is so; it is necessary that society actually provide for a kind of education that will always preserve the possibility of peaceful change.

The essential purpose of any educational system remains the preservation of society, but "preservation" must be defined very broadly if it is not to come to mean only the desperate shoring-up of a self-destructive status quo. American higher education, being the servant of a society that is at once immensely complex and profoundly insecure, has too often allowed its purpose to be interpreted in this narrow, futile sense. The result is what I have called "sectarianism," which we might examine under four of its closely related—and often overlapping—aspects.

The first is simple academic conservatism. By that I mean

that combination of fear of reproach from the community and professional smugness that makes administrators—and, especially, boards of trustees—reluctant to hire teachers who, though possessing academic credentials, are thought to be out of the "mainstream" of wholesome thought. This kind of conservatism is manifested in state universities as an intolerance of "subversives," in Catholic universities as an intolerance of non-Catholics or liberal Catholics, in small rural colleges as an intolerance of "leftists," and so on. Some of this intolerance arises from personal conviction, some from economic necessity. Our universities are dependent upon their benefactors—whether they be church, state, alumni or what have you—and those groups, the mainstays of the Establishment, are likely to demand that the money they contribute will not be used to undermine the social order. Although that expectation is sometimes conservative in the good sense, its effects are nearly always conservative in the bad sense.

It is this fact that most offends the idealism of students who feel that the university should be independent of the society that supports it and a critic of its failings. There are few experiences as disillusioning—or as illuminating to the idealist —as that of students who are told by a university administrator that he agrees with their call for some reform or other but that "the alumni wouldn't stand for it." Students demand more courage from administrators. Of course, courage is not a quality that can be evoked upon demand; rather, they should press for the end of a system by which universities depend for their existence upon handouts from individuals whose interests may conflict with the universities' independence. The financial problem is *the* problem facing American higher education, and the arguments pro and con government funding are complex and compelling.

A second flaw of our universities is their functionalism. It is no accident that they have been termed "knowledge factories" designed to turn out saleable products. Academic disciplines are considered valuable to the extent that they turn out professionally useful people. Our system of graduate schools demonstrates that the only kind of serious postgraduate study that one can do at a university is study designed to produce scholars and teachers, in that order. It is sometimes permitted but usually frowned upon for one to take postgraduate courses merely out of interest in them. Private high schools like to stress that they are "college preparatory;" but colleges are merely graduate school preparatory and graduate schools career preparatory. Most students do expect that their education will prepare them for their careers, and universities would be failing one of their important responsibilities if they did not provide this opportunity. That education should prepare one for a career, however, does not mean that it should do nothing else; yet many of our university curricula are based on the presumption that every course must promise to prove "useful" in the future, and those that do not are often weeded out.

This kind of functionalism is least excusable at the liberal arts end of the academic scale; but even in the professional schools, where it has more justification, functionalism often runs rampant. An example will point up the extent of its influence. In my first year at the Yale Law School a majority of my classmates requested that grading be abolished, in favor of a system in which students could only pass or fail each course. A faculty committee was set up to examine the question, and after weeks of study and meetings with all concerned it recommended that the grading scheme of the school be revised. The idea of a pass-fail system was rejected as educationally irresponsible, since students deserved to have their work more thoroughly evaluated than that system would allow; but it was agreed that the present system of standard letter-grades and rank-in-class was arbitary and perhaps meaningless. Their revision would have abolished class rankings and reduced the number of grading categories so that only broad degrees of quality would be delineated.

When their recommendation came before the faculty for a vote, it was rejected, largely on the basis of reports that the legal profession expected the school to give the traditional kind of grades to aid the employer in evaluating its graduates and that a change in grading practice might make it more difficult for graduates of the school to secure jobs. Most of the students agreed with the faculty, once they were told that their careers might be hurt by a change. Of course, many faculty members felt that the older system was more sound educationally; but a majority of those voting to preserve it, including some who felt that the proposed system was academically superior, were responding to what they imagined were the demands of the profession. A year later the proposal was adopted after further study; but no one who was involved in the dispute, whether pro or con, would deny that there was a surge of functionalist feeling when the proposal was first made. This is a perfect case of a functionalist pressure on educational policy because it is an explicit one; but there are many more subtle, and probably more destructive, ways in which our universities respond to pressure from non-academic sources which measure the university's success in terms of the ability of its graduates to function within the social system they represent.

A third flaw is authoritarianism. According to many administrators, students are in school to be taught by their knowledgeable elders and, consequently, have no role to play in the formation of university policy. The proposition is contradictory, of course, since students would surely learn more from playing a responsible role in the formation of university policy. Use of this specious argument by university administrators has been a sore point for both faculty and students. Faculty members have won increasing influence in most American universities; but the students' voice is only now being taken seriously, and in most places "student power" is still far from becoming a fact.

The distribution of power within the university is crucial to all the criticisms students make of their education because the fate of such criticism depends upon the influence of students in the decision-making apparatus. Although it would not be true to say that if students had more power, the university would necessarily enact reforms in the direction of student demands, it would necessarily have some effect. In the grading dispute at Yale Law School both students and faculty were more cowed by outside pressure than administrators were. However, broadening of the power base would necessarily lead to more diversity of thought and policy, and diversity is the counter force to sectarianism.

The last aspect of this sectarianism is educational Darwinism. This theory, upon which most of our educational system is founded, sees school as an elaborate contest in which the quick succeed and are assigned to an appropriate form of successful life-style after completing the course. The slow, including those who are only distracted from the prospect of success for a time, are assigned to failure. This theory results in an array of exams, marks, standardized tests and enough hours of homework to make childhood an experience no sensitive adult could endure without cracking up. Few children do crack up but that is because they are too young to know what is being stolen from them.

Competition has perverted education in many ways. For

one thing, it has caused it to be directed too much toward the future. The purpose of study in any one grade of school is to get promoted to the next grade, and so on all the way up to promotion from college into a "good" job. The effect of this is to put a premium on those kinds of study that will help one to advance and to discourage those that will not. The result is that the kinds of learning which are most easily measurable become the most important. The more personal and creative areas of education suffer: students have very little time, and it is tempting not to spend any of it on things that intellectually fascinate, if studying something else will help on the next exam. The net result is to push education toward an emphasis on the objective to the point where learning comes to mean learning facts.

There might be some validity to this in grammar school and high school where students are attempting to master basic subjects and skills. In college, however, the reduction of education to the accumulation of information is futile and academically mediocre. The system may have worked several decades ago; but today there is simply too much to learn, too many fields of study whose surfaces can barely be penetrated in a few short years of college. No one today can learn even the fundamentals of all the more common disciplines at college. This fact has been reluctantly recognized, but the peddlers of information have proposed the wrong solution: that each student specialize earlier and more exclusively, if only so that he will learn a lot about *something*.

This reminds me of the way we were taught religion in high school and of the old theology curricula. For years we thought of religion as a collection of facts that we were expected to believe. That kind of religion has been largely rejected by my generation in favor of a religion that emphasizes action which reflects the religious reality. Students crave the same kind of transformation of their secular education. The new religion centers around morality in the sense of discriminate action; and students want their education to prepare them for the same thing, although morality would probably not be a word they would use. In a situation like the present one where there is too much to be learned on campus, a critical sense of high quality must be instilled. This kind of education, which lasts a lifetime, will take care of itself. The intellectually curious have always taught themselves, and universities can best fulfill their role in this age by teaching the skills that will make such learning possible.

Obviously, the university which will succeed at this task will be the one that promotes searching criticism of all kinds—of itself and of society. The crux of today's student revolt is the demand that universities stop making it their business to prove in a hundred different ways that ours is the best of all possible nations, churches or schools. Universities should turn their attention to probing the question of what a good nation, church or school ought to be. Student power is essential to this demand because for students to learn to be responsibly critical they must have the freedom to make mistakes. Without the power to formulate, execute and criticize policy, development of a mature critical sense is impossible. No one ever learned to drive while sitting in the back seat, no matter how valid and illuminating the lecture from the front might be.

3

from politics
to the movement

The 1960's ushered in the first possibility of political change. The apparent triumph of youth and energy over the inertia of the Eisenhower era by the election of John F. Kennedy seemed more than victory—it was liberation. In our eyes the Kennedy program was a vindication of political activism and a death blow to social inertia. Those of us who had felt out of joint before—in school, church, or politics—immediately became "liberals." Liberalism seemed the glorification of intelligence over experience and so came quite naturally to the young.

The spirit of the Kennedy administration was contagious. His victory at the polls had been *our* victory and he consciously enlisted us in his cause. We were not old enough to

have achieved political sophistication, but we were young
enough to distrust our elders and the elderly air of the Eisenhower administration. President Kennedy caught on so
quickly among young people, not because he said things that
we had never heard, but because he said the sorts of things to
the nation that we had begun to say to each other. It was an
immense relief, as well as a cause for excitement, to discover
that the head of our government knew the kinds of questions
we were asking and even seemed to want to answer them.

As politics moved from the periphery to the center of our
lives we searched for ways to express our new-found faith. For
the many of us who were too young to vote, organized politics
was a reality we had barely glimpsed. In any case we wanted
to test our ideas and energies. Since there was no way to
participate in what was happening in Washington, we looked
for work closer to home. The civil rights movement, which
had begun its quiet and forceful growth in the previous decade, now became the rallying-point of our liberalism. The civil
rights movement, we believed, offered us an opportunity to
make the promise of America real. All the self-congratulatory
rhetoric of our Cold War foreign policy depended for its truth
upon the outcome of that struggle; because, if we failed, the
rest of the world might call us liars. The civil rights question
attracted us because it seemed so clear-cut. One section of the
country—the most educationally backward, least industrialized, least urbanized and least sophisticated—was inflicting
systematic racial discrimination upon some of its citizens.
How could we condemn totalitarianism abroad when in parts
of America local governments had set up virtual equivalents
of the police-state?

The impulse to support the movement turned out to be
quite different from working in it. Stories of sit-ins in the Deep
South had romantic appeal for the students who stayed home

and tried to find ways to participate in the great crusade. They were anything but romantic for the students who actually went down South and sat in. These discovered a world they would not have believed could exist in America. Middle-class students found themselves for the first time in their lives fearing the police. They found themselves in a situation where government, order, and society itself were enemies to be distrusted and thwarted if possible. Not many Americans live through such an experience, and the young who did had their conception of freedom altered forever by it.

Not many students actually went to the South, but a great many were involved in one way or another in the struggle for civil rights. They were the backbone of the student political activity that followed, although student generations follow each other so rapidly that perhaps a majority of the students now in college were not directly involved in the civil rights fight. The civil rights movement fathered the politics of my generation. It gave us our first look at politics—the confrontation between people and government and the distribution of power between them—and it served as the training-ground for the development of our political style. In the civil rights movement we gave America a chance. The moral issue was clearcut, solutions seemed evident, if not easy; and the weight of public opinion and government power was on our side. America mobilized her conscience, her power and the energies of her youth, and then America failed.

As liberals we had inherited the trappings of liberalism and of the Democratic Party. We believed in the irresistible power of the federal government to right wrongs. We believed that what our nation told the rest of the world about freedom here was substantially true and that the American system was the embodiment of political liberty. We thought that the cause of American black people would enlist the support of everyone

but the Ku Klux Klan and that concerted effort would bring
about rapid integration and economic advancement for
blacks. The optimism of those days was not merely the naïvete
of our youth. It was the simplest assertion of our faith in
America and a demand for the minimum fulfillment of the
American ideal. If we are now in the winter of our discontent,
its spring was the failure of the civil rights movement.

That failure signalled the beginning of the transformation
of our notions about American politics. The first shock was the
discovery of the pervasiveness of racism and of the average
American's terror of black people which would prevent him
from sharing power or freedom with them. Indeed, we learned
that his fear of black people led him to consciously deny them
those prerequisites of full citizenship. The second shock was
the ineffectuality of government. All the laws we asked for
were passed, but nothing happened. We learned that the
problem was not isolated in one section of the country but that
the special conditions of the South made its racism more obvious. The more sophisticated racism of the urban and suburban
North revealed itself as more threatening and far more significant for the future of our black population.

At the same time the struggle began to change from within.
As the goals of the movement changed, so did the place of
white liberals within it. I do not remember this gradual exclu-
sion of whites as the kind of reverse racism it is usually depicted. The call for black power was a logical reaction to the
failure of white power to solve or even understand the problem of racism. The first drives for national attention, massive
sympathy and federal legislation had demanded the combined
efforts of blacks and whites because this phase was directed
toward the white community. Civil rights leaders felt that if
they could win the sympathy of a great many white people,

racism, at least in its institutionalized forms, would be eliminated. The black men and women who spearheaded the drive
were a small and courageous minority who placed their lives
in jeopardy by directly confronting white power. At first, they
made no attempt to enlist the active support of the entire black
community. Instead, they fought small-scale racism in sit-ins
and demonstrations to exert pressure upon the government
and white citizens. Their aim was to change laws and correct
social injustice.

But when new legislation failed to effect significant change,
and many whites reacted against full equality for blacks, the
militants changed their strategy. White America proved unwilling to risk a massive and irreversible change. Blacks
realized that only a much stronger black community could
make change a reality. Pride and cohesion had to be instilled
into a people who had been degraded for centuries. Whites
could not play a leading role in this new effort. White men
telling black men they should be more proud would worsen,
not cure, the racist dilemma.

At the same time, white students who had been deeply involved in the civil rights movement now found themselves cut
off from an important part of their lives. They had already
become more and more disenchanted with their country. They
no longer believed there was "liberty and justice for all" in
America. Most Americans seemed anxious to preserve their
privileges despite consequent injustice to blacks. The discovery of this intolerance in their own middle-class communities estranged white students from the society from which
they came. Many of them looked upon themselves as outcasts,
and they began to identify strongly with the outcast black
community. Black resolution to be independent left white students without a group with which they could identify and no

role to play. To overcome their alienation, they began the organization of their own community—the university campus.

The movement of white students out of the militant civil rights organizations was hastened by increasing activity in the areas of foreign policy and peace. Most young people, I think, were fed up with the Cold War after the election of President Kennedy. They were tired of living with the constant threat of a war that everyone professed not to want. This longing for *peace*—not an armed truce—did not immediately take the form of criticism of the belligerence of American policy. They had been well schooled to believe that Communism was the only threat to peace and that the Cold War would end when the Communists finally admitted the necessity for co-existence. The students believed that America's aggressive foreign policy was designed to convince the Soviet Union, and later, China, that they could not dominate the world and that as soon as they gave up their ambitions to do so peace could be achieved.

Students soon began to realize that international politics was not that simple. A common assumption of their childhood had been that Russia was in the grip of a bloody totalitarian dictatorship which suppressed by ruthless police-state methods the desire of the Russian people for freedom. Communists, they thought, were men so intrinsicially evil and so entranced by the vision of power that they would stop at nothing to attain it. It did not take long for well-informed students to see that this simply was not the case. They saw that the Stalin era had passed and that many Russians were apparently content with their form of government. They realized that the leaders of the Communist countries were sincere, and so they began to listen to what they said with interest mixed with a good deal of skepticism.

An example will illustrate how this realization altered their thinking about American foreign policy. Students were appalled, along with the rest of the nation, when President Kennedy revealed that Soviet missiles were being set up in Cuba. It seemed natural that the United States should do everything in her power to prevent the establishment of hostile military bases just ninety miles off her shores. But after the tension of the crisis had subsided, we thought more deeply about it. The United States had completely surrounded the Soviet Union with bases. Our forces in Turkey, for example, enjoyed the same strategic position that a Soviet base in Cuba would have. Yet the Soviet Union did not blockade the ports of our European allies and insist that we keep our forces at home. It became clear, then, that there was a certain amount of doublethink inherent in America's righteous indignation.

For many students this was a momentous change in their thinking. For the first time they separated their nation's behavior from its propaganda. When they did, they began to see that the black-and-white polarizations of Cold War rhetoric failed to convey the real meaning of the tension between East and West. Disputes were dressed up by the antagonists in ideological trappings but were really exercises of national interest. The United States did not want missiles in Cuba and was willing to risk war to keep them out. Whether it was consistent or inconsistent, moral or immoral, to take that risk was irrelevant. Once young people saw that ideology was not as large a factor in our foreign policy as they had been taught to believe, they refused to accept any longer that every anti-Communist tactic was justified. With the ideological blinders removed from their eyes, they began to analyze Soviet and American policy more objectively.

The result was a conviction that there was a good deal of

evil on both sides of the Cold War. Both blocs worked for
their national interests in a way that abused the freedom of
other nations. The Soviet Union ruthlessly crushed the Hun-
garian revolt to maintain her traditional hegemony in eastern
Europe. The United States supported an invasion of Cuba and
fostered anti-revolutionary forces in South America to protect
its vast commercial interests there. The Soviet Union *was* governed under a totalitarian system, but we supported totalitarian
governments all over the world provided that they were
pledged to support America's interests. When students saw
how these conflicting interests made pawns of weaker nations, they came to believe that the chief enemy of peace in the
world was not Communism or capitalism but the self-perpetu-
ating Cold War itself.

They realized that commercialism and nationalistic power
politics governed both sides. One major problem was that the
ideological basis of American foreign policy—all the talk of
the international Communist conspiracy—had been bandied
about for so long that it was believed, not only by the American people generally, but by many in government, too. This
was so true that pragmatic solutions were sometimes impossible because of American ideology and Americans' failure to
understand the real position of the other side. Students wondered whether President Kennedy would have acted so force-
fully as he did in the Cuban missile crisis if he had not believed
that the Russians realized that they had tried to pull a dirty
trick and had failed and so would not take a strong stand
when confronted by force. The war in Vietnam provided
many more examples to teach young people that ideology can
make effective political action difficult.

As many students lost their early faith in the ideological
purity of America, they substituted, not pragmatism, but

idealism with a new emphasis. This frequently took the form of sympathy for the nations of the under-developed world which were often disastrously caught between the clashing interests of the East and West. It led students to condemn the tactics of both sides when they operated against the interests of the "third world." The weakness of this dealistic position was that it made communication with their own government difficult. Government officials who were ideologues considered students who denied their Cold War presumptions disloyal. The pragmatists were unmoved by calls to shape American policy in the interests of other nations, instead of solely in the interests of America.

For most Catholics there was no question that the Cold War was exactly what the U.S. government leaders had always said it was—all-out war between the forces of freedom and slavery. I remember being struck by the similarity in pre-Vatican II Catholic attitudes toward Protestants and Communists. When we were younger, we had been taught that Protestant "error" was self-evident and that even a Catholic high school freshman could win any religious debate with a Protestant. The same kind of attitude was common towards Communists. Although few Catholics I knew had ever met a Communist, they thought that Communists were insincere. They thought that Communists were possessed by a lust for power and power was all they knew or cared about. I suspect that my increasing contacts with Protestants during high school and the realization that they were not what we had been taught to expect encouraged my early attempts to try to understand the Cold War, if only to learn how to oppose it. Anyone who has studied the Reformation must believe that the most trenchant ideological clashes could eventually dissolve into awkward harmony. The increasing interest in ecu-

menism in the early 60's made the parallel interest in peaceful
co-existence with Communism more plausible and promising.

Two problems confronted all student activists: they wished
to communicate both with the government and the people of
the country. The government had to be convinced that the
public wanted more frankness and less propaganda from their
officials; the public had to be convinced that the Cold War was
unnecessary and dangerous and that more attention should be
paid to the creation of foreign aid without political strings.
Because students framed their position in terms hostile to the
Cold War, dialogue with either group was difficult. The public
was still mired in the Cold War mentality, and many officials
became victims of their own attempts at indoctrination.
Liberals who had always fought for foreign aid as an anti-
Communist measure found themselves unable to secure foreign aid unless it could be shown to have definite anti-Communist strategic value.

Most students used the peace movement as a means of communication with the government and the nation as a whole.
The movement had been in existence for years, but its first real
popular strength developed in the early 60's in the campaign
to end testing of nuclear weapons in the atmosphere. It is easy
to forget what those years were like. (When was the last time
we heard anyone mention a fallout shelter?). Yet these were
the years when nuclear war seemed almost likely, and the
desperate frenzy of the civil defense mentality swept the nation. There was talk of building bomb shelters in backyards,
and of arming them for defense against neighbors who might
seek refuge in time of attack. Larger and larger bombs were
exploded in the atmosphere, despite evidence that the level of
radioactive fallout had risen dangerously. The peace movement during this period was a small group of people who

dared to say aloud that civil defense was futile and falsely
reassuring since both East and West possessed large enough
nuclear arsenals to guarantee each other's utter destruction.
The early forms of protest usually centered around civil dis-
obedience during air raid drills. The demonstrations caused so
much disorder in New York, at least, that drills were discontinued, depriving this decade's school children of a valuable
but grim reminder of what the "balance of terror" means.

The ranks of the peace movement swelled quickly in the
early 60's. Some of the increase can be accounted for by the
disintegration of the mass-movement aspects of the civil rights
struggle. Thousands of students who had been mobilized in
that battle turned to the peace movement to express their indignation at the state of the world they were to inherit. The
Cuban missile crisis brought home the real possibility of sudden all-out war. The conflict in Laos and America's slowly
escalating involvement in Vietnam underlined the danger of a
policy based on interventionism and the repression of revolution. Student loyalties to the people of the third world were
heightened by the sensitivity to exploitation acquired in the
civil rights movement. Students became more and more aware
that the great powers not only manipulated domestic policies
of poor nations but even threatened the very existence of small
countries by "wars of national liberation."

Like the civil rights movement the peace movement was
concerned with communication but in quite different ways.
The early civil rights movement had focused a clear-cut moral
and legal issue, and the greatest difficulty lay in getting people
to overcome feelings that, in many cases, they were already
ashamed of. Until the appearance of the blacklash—that is,
until the effort reached the North—most Americans were
strongly sympathetic with at least the goals of the struggle. But

the peace movement started from a different point altogether. Its premise was that American foreign policy was misdirected and that much of our government's Cold War rhetoric was inaccurate and even deceitful. This was not easy for most Americans to accept. The plight of blacks in our nation was more evident than the failure of our foreign policy, even if neither had been very widely recognized.

The peace movement was doomed to its own kind of failure, and it came more surely and more emphatically than the failure of the fight for civil rights. Disillusionment with the ability of national legislation to insure equality for blacks had led to a movement for dignity and strength within the black community, but the peace movement could have no other object than a change in government policy. There was no community to turn back to, except perhaps the academic community; but universities had been allies from the beginning, and that did not seem to alter policy very much. In the face of continuing escalation of the war, the movement could only repeat its futile tactics with greater intensity and with more and more desperation. It is true that eventually a majority of the American people did come to see that the war in Vietnam was, if nothing else, a blunder, and this was certainly largely due to the efforts of the movement. But I am talking now not about 1968, but about 1965 and 1966, when attempts were still being made to speak directly to the government and when government policy was becoming increasingly rigid and uncompromising.

The result of our failure to make headway in those years, in short, was another transformation of our notion of how America needed to be changed, and provoked the emergence of what has been called the New Left.

It is only necessary for our present purposes to explain the significance of the formation of the New Left in terms of the forces that have already been described. Those forces were principally the apparent failure of liberalism to achieve peace abroad and equal justice at home, and the effect of its failure on the political consciousness of the young people who had placed their faith in liberalism's promise.

I do not think that the assassination of President Kennedy was seen at first as a blow to the movement. We all had our doubts about President Johnson at the beginning, but his early success with Congress, following the floundering of the Kennedy legislative program, reassured us that government was still on the right track. The election of 1964 was decisive because it indicated that the American people at large agreed with us. President Kennedy had been narrowly elected and had been resisted by a hesitant Congress from the start of his term in office. Now President Johnson's program was being attacked outright by a man who stood opposed to all the values we had discovered in the past few years. The overwhelming defeat of Barry Goldwater's naked conservatism was a great boost to our morale and an incentive to greater political activity. With his decisive popular mandate in hand, President Johnson spurred on his war on poverty toward the achievement of a Great Society.

This was the high point of youth's confidence in the government and in the intentions of the American people. We were still riding high on the enthusiasm that had been generated by John Kennedy even though we had become doubtful of the wisdom of American foreign policy. The important point is that we were still willing to work with what we considered to be the better elements in the government. Many of us were involved in President Johnson's campaign for election. Others swelled the ranks of the Peace Corps and VISTA, and stu-

dents who went abroad often found themselves defending
America against the criticisms levelled against her everywhere. This was no longer the simplistic bravado of the early
days of the civil rights movement. Students knew that there
was a lot of work to be done at home and that the struggle for
peace and equal rights would be an uphill one. But it was felt
that a watershed had been reached in 1964 and that the conscience of America had decided at last to take the right path,
even if at a slower pace than we would have liked.

Perhaps only such great hope could have led to such acute
disappointment. Civil rights legislation was enacted, and the
plight of the average black man was not affected in the least.
Despite the promise of military restraint, the war in Vietnam
gnawed away at funds for domestic programs until the much-
touted programs of the Great Society were nothing but
elaborate and empty promises. The issue of priorities in national spending came to the forefront, and guns won every
round over butter. Most disturbing of all to students was the
knowledge that it was not conservatives but men who called
themselves liberals who were responsible. It became apparent,
therefore, that liberalism was not enough, that it was not providing the answers that America needed to extricate herself
from the plagues of war and racism. But our upbringing provided us with no alternatives to liberalism save Conservatism,
Socialism, and Communism.

All the political concerns of student activists in the mid-60's,
when examined, can be reduced to a concern for freedom.
Our sympathy with underdeveloped nations was a desire that
their freedom of self-determination be preserved despite the
tug-of-war being fought over them by East and West so that
they might move on to free themselves, with America's help,
from poverty and colonialism. Our work in the civil rights

movement was aimed directly at securing freedom for black
people from the slavery of economic and political deprivation.
Our attacks on the sectarianism of universities was a call for
greater academic freedom and for the freeing of students from
the conservatism and authoritarianism that denied them any
role in the formation of university policy. Our opposition to
the draft was a defense of the freedom of young men not to be
forced to fight for a cause they could not believe in, a defense
of the freedom of every man from forced labor. In all these
cases, we were demonstrating a fear that personal freedom
would be lost amidst the competing claims of big government,
big business, big labor, mass education, mass communications
and mass society.

Traditionally, the American conservative movement has
rather illogically claimed that concern for individual freedom
was its monopoly. Indeed, conservatism enjoyed a vogue
among some students in the early 60's who were reacting to
many of the same fears that I have just described. But conservatism could not capture the loyalty of a majority of students, because its claim to the defense of freedom was clearly
belied by practical contradictions. Despite all their talk about
the defense of the individual, for example, conservatives ignored the deprivation of individual rights suffered by blacks in
the South; they supported the suppression of free speech for
Communists and Leftists; claimed that the self-interest of the
United States was more important than the right of under-
developed nations to self-determination and called for the dilution of the legal rights of persons accused of crime.

In fact, conservative political philosophy was based on a
selective defense of freedom. A white man should be "free"
not to sell a house to a black man; but a black man should not
be "free" to live wherever he can afford to. Conservatives

82   *from politics to the movement*

opposed "big government" and "big labor," but were seldom critical of "big business." Conservatives were for the most part interested in preserving the freedom of the already powerful and did not concern themselves with the freedom of the weak. They did not deny the right of an accused man to say nothing and call his lawyer if arrested, since that is a right the rich would know about and exercise. They merely insisted that the police were being abused if required to inform the poor that they have the same right. The conservative emphasis on "freedom" was perhaps sincere; but it applied only to a very narrowly defined freedom. This very narrowness explains in part the great enthusiasm for conservatism among lower middle class Catholic students who hope to graduate soon into a class that conservative political philosophy is designed to protect. The portrait of the St. John's University student in *Crisis at St. John's* provides one explanation. The authors state,

. . . it is not unreasonable to assume that in New York City, many Negroes and Catholics are also in direct economic conflict. A number of Catholic intellectuals suppose this to be the reason that the church in New York waited so long to take a stand on civil rights. . . . The overwhelming majority of students at St. John's have taken a negative stand.*

Socialism might have been more attractive to disillusioned liberal students, if it had not failed to meet their criticisms of America squarely. Socialists in this country were disunited and failed to provide a clear program for change. Moreover, the experience of young people with the war in Vietnam had built a new distrust of government power; and socialists too

* Joseph Scimecca and Roland Damiano, *Crisis at St. John's* (New York: Random House, 1967), p. 100.

often couched their programs in terms of taking all power away from business and giving it to government. At least most people thought they did. It did not matter that most Socialists were ardent Democrats. Students had seen enough government manipulation of facts about the war and pressure against dissent to wonder how an even more powerful government could be resisted, even with the right to vote intact. Certain versions of Syndicalism, a decentralized system whereby labor unions owned factories, seemed to promise greater freedom but had no prospect of success in present-day America and not much of an audience among students. A good deal of Socialist theory was built upon glorification of the worker, but our work for civil rights and peace had convinced us that America's prosperous workers were often the most conservative citizens. We were interested in securing a measure of power for the lower classes, not for the already-dominant middle class. Besides, Socialism as a movement seemed terribly dull, and even old-fashioned, when we considered its tired performance in Western Europe and its consistent failure to inspire this country.

It is difficult to discuss "Communism" as though it were really a single distinct form of politics. We had been raised to associate the term with the Soviet form of government, and the totalitarianism of that system made it unattractive to almost all activists. Other "Communisms" that had sprung up in the underdeveloped world were regarded with interest and often with sympathy. Ho's system in North Vietnam and Castro's in Cuba seemed superior to what had preceded them. Like most revolutionary governments, these depended upon a degree of authoritarianism that we found unappealing; but at any rate, there were few who thought that those experiments had very much to teach the United States. Sympathy among students for certain figures associated with the Communist sphere should not be mistaken for a feeling that their policies should be adopted by this country. Many students liked Mao because he gave power to the young and Che Guevara because he had the courage to do what others did not dare; but in most cases—though of course not all—this was not so much an expression of politics as of sympathy with a kindred idealism.

In fact, the more perceptive students were not looking for an ideology to substitute for anti-Communism. They realized the danger inherent in all ideologies—the slow growth of dogmatism and death of openness to other ways of thinking. If there was anything that the experience of the previous few years had taught them, it was that it was not an ideology, but an approach to all ideologies, that was needed. Liberalism had filled that role, but it had so ensnared itself in Cold War rhetoric to sell itself to the conservative American public that many liberals lost the ability to disbelieve their own propaganda. Moreover, liberalism had been the established doctrine in American politics since 1932 and should not really have been expected to renovate itself radically since no established group ever does. Liberals were still overly-fascinated with the ability of the federal government to solve problems, a fascination which had begun, understandably, in the New Deal era but which had remained unmodified by the lessons of this decade. Liberalism, tied as it was to the Democratic Party—which, to retain its broad support, must advocate only very conservative reform—seemed completely unable to provide a vehicle for the kind of change we sought.

Our concern was freedom, but we saw that freedom had more meanings than we had been taught. We knew that in most Communist countries freedom of speech, press, assembly and religion were curtailed to varying degrees and that destroyed any romantic illusions about the liberating power of Communism. But we saw at the same time that many Americans were not economically free, and that there was proportionately more poverty in the United States than in any other industrialized Western nation. A right to employment has been written into the constitutions of many new nations, but in America economic freedom is not considered one of the essentials of liberty. Again, students in the Soviet Union may advance in their studies as far as their talents will take them. For many in the United States money alone can buy a higher education. In South America, students exercise much more power within the university structure than American students do. England has for decades carefully protected the rights of those accused of crimes, while our Supreme Court is vilified by conservative Americans for enforcing the most basic requirements of due process. We became convinced, then, that while the American system remained in many ways one of the more democratic, there was room for much improvement before we could honestly present ourselves to the world as *the* model to be followed.

The conviction that freedom was too complicated an idea to be reduced to a single formula led students to reject the political theories offered to the world by the United States and the Communist bloc. The American theory was individualism: if each individual strove to perfect himself, and was left free to do so, society would develop most rapidly. The reply of the other side was Communism: if every individual subordinated himself to the needs of the community, society would develop most rapidly. Neither philosophy adequately provides for the fulfillment of the *person*, who in one system might be destroyed by failure in the individualist rat race, and in the other be submerged in the communal ant heap.

The personalism of the student New Left, in contrast, emphasizes the necessity that *each* person be allowed to fulfill himself by being freed from manipulation and exploitation of every kind. The New Left is accused of having no ideology when in fact it has an ideology but no program. Most student activists have not decided that there is a single system that will best provide for the protection of the person. The New Left has not been quick to suggest a replacement for our entire culture, nor would it be wise to try to tie down its personalist concern to a single mode of political formation. Most student New Leftists want to fight manipulation where they find it. This can be done in the United States by working for more power for black people, and it can be done in Czechoslovakia by loosening the hold of the Soviet Union over internal affairs. New Leftists, exemplified by Students for a Democratic Society (SDS), have called for the establishment of "participatory democracy" in this country; and that call, since it stresses that persons be allowed to participate fully in the institutions which affect their lives, has many practical implications: decentralization of many institutions, for example. But the outlines are vague and that is evidence of a certain political maturity. The personalism of the student New Left is not a system but a standard by which any system may be judged. It is the only philosophy of politics which does not call for the destruction of all other political philosophies but merely for their reform.

One might well ask whether personalism is a political philosophy at all. I would suggest that it is not but that it grew out of our experience of politics. Actually, it is a kind of moral philosophy; but I think that many student activists, fed up as they are with what they see as the hypocrisy of organized religion, would not like to hear it called that. Indeed, I wonder whether many of them call it personalism. I choose to, but there is no consensus around that term, or any term, or even around the elements of the attitude it attempts to describe. Indeed, it would be grossly deceptive for me to pretend that all, or even most, students who consider themselves to be members of the New Left would agree with my analysis of their position. Student political activism is in a crisis in this country. Strong forces—a good number of police forces, for example—pull in the direction of more or less violent action. The student population of America and the influences upon it are extremely diverse. The meaning which I have drawn from their political history culminating in what I would call the personalist consciousness is true to the extent that this is what happened in the lives of many of us. I also think—and hope—that it is the implication of the more advanced student thinking of the last few years.

Certainly, personalism was a very conscious element in the most recent major phase in my generation's political odyssey, the McCarthy campaign. Eugene McCarthy often spoke of the "personalist concern" of the young, and the program he advocated was a perfect example of the sort of program "personalists" could support. His position came under attack from both liberals and conservatives because it was not patterned exclusively after either of their theories. Liberals were aroused over McCarthy's call for decentralization of government, and conservatives were in arms over his refusal to indulge in any empty Cold War rhetoric whatever. What he called for was that the distance between citizen and government be shortened, that institutions be given back to the people, that manipulation of weaker nations in our "national interest" be ended and that the poor of this nation be provided for without

insult to their dignity and freedom. These are the directions in
which the activist young would have their country move; and
the failure of Eugene McCarthy's campaign has disturbing
implications which will be discussed after the sketch of the
background of my generation has been completed by a discussion of the development of their religion.

4

religion and rebellion

It is more dangerous to generalize about the religious development of a group of individuals than it is to outline their political development because religious experience, which is in many ways more personal, is less susceptible to accurate observation. This does not mean that generalizations cannot be made nor that they will not be; but if it was necessary in the last two chapters to allow for wide divergence in individual cases, it is doubly so in this one. Again my conclusions will be based on the experience of Catholic students whom I know best. Catholics are institutionally at closer quarters than most Protestants are, and it is hard for any of them to move without everyone feeling it. The shifts within that church are more explicit and easier to describe as a result. Although Ca-

tholicism will be used illustratively, these remarks are not addressed solely to Catholics. The features of Catholicism which
are crucial here—its sectarianism, for example, or its emphasis on salvation—are common to most Christian churches,
and I imagine that most students react in the same way to
these common features.

Religion has three essential aspects. The spiritual aspect is
closely bound up with worship; for Catholics, this means the
sacraments, especially participation in the Eucharist. The doc-
trinal aspect of religion is a particular set of beliefs about God
and man and the relationship between them. The moral aspect embodies the demand that believers act in certain
ways. It seems to me that the religious experience of my
generation has passed through three phases, in each of which
one of these aspects was stressed to the detriment of the
others. In our childhood we thought of religion as something
to be practiced in church; in adolescence it was something to
be believed; and now in early adulthood we see it as something to be lived. This evolution needs to be examined in
some detail.

Some of the qualities of our childhood religion can be in-
ferred from the earlier discussion of education. In grammar
school we were taught to regard ourselves as a Catholic
minority in a hostile Protestant country, but the insecurity of
feeling ourselves a minority was more than balanced by the
conviction that the position of our church was absolutely
correct. This elitism was an important facet of the "siege
mentality," and was fed by the belief that our church alone
among churches could guarantee the truth of all its doctrines.
Since Catholics were not in fact persecuted in America, the
defensiveness and fear that had led to the development of the
siege mentality easily gave way to a joyful chauvinism. We

had the feeling as children that we really had it made, as though we had a special secret promise of a future of eternal happiness in heaven.

The religion of our childhood was chiefly characterized by this emphasis on salvation. Life on earth was totally directed toward the attainment of life in heaven, and since this made life on earth a means, not an end, it led to a certain other-worldliness in our approach to human problems. With our eyes fixed on heaven, close inspection of the earth was difficult. It might seem that this salvational emphasis would at least have had a salutary effect on morals, but the thrust of grammar school religion was largely non-moral. Heaven was a reward for faithful adherence to religious practice. For young Catholics this meant that as long as we obeyed the laws of the Church with regard to the sacraments, we were assured of salvation—provided, of course, that we remained free of serious sin. Such sin, fortunately, was not easy to commit. We were taught that one would not be held accountable for his immoral acts unless he were fully conscious of their immorality when he committed them. It was difficult for us in those days to imagine ourselves that consciously evil, and so we presumed that there was little doubt that we would be saved so long as we fulfilled the requirements of devotional practice.

I do not mean this as a purely negative criticism. These rules were not just regimentation nor one more attempt by the church to keep its children as firmly in its grasp as possible. Our teachers recognized that the sacraments are essential to the preservation of the whole atmosphere of Catholicism itself, as they knew it. The motive was not to expand the mood of Catholic churches, the spell cast by candles, incense and vestments. They knew, on the contrary, that continual awareness of the spiritual requires constant practice; the soul needs exercise. The regular practice of religion by Catholic youngsters, when it is more than an habitual reflex, has the effect of creating and maintaining a world of the spirit that might otherwise go unperceived. Regular reception of the sacraments, or even attendance at church, can be a source of strength to maintain morality and foster reflection and self-examination. In short, the emphasis on worship in our early training had the great advantage of creating a strong sense of the spiritual. Such emphasis was not misplaced.

We were too young to understand theology and too innocent to appreciate morality. Worship was substantially the whole of our religion. On the other hand, we were taught a good deal about God and about the church; and we accepted all that we were taught in the same way that we accepted what we were told about history and arithmetic. Even this naive faith, however, received its sustenance from liturgical practice, as I very early learned. When I was thirteen I stopped receiving the sacraments for a while because of a scheduling conflict between Mass and a movie in which the movie won. Once outside the atmosphere of the church, everything looked astoundingly different, and for the first time some of the things I had been told seemed less than convincing. I do not pretend that at that age I was prepared to refute the theological underpinnings of my faith—I was really just indulging the sophistication of a thirteen-year-old atheist. But my belief in the way of life defined by Catholicism was severely strained by a lapse in religious practice.

This sort of rebellion against the church in early adolescence was fairly common among my contemporaries and was probably just one part of the usual adolescent revolt against authority. In most cases it did not seem to have permanent effects on those of us who continued in Catholic schools. I had decided to attend a Catholic high school because I believed the Catholic educational system in New York superior to the public schools. Many of my classmates were not given a choice but were sent to Catholic schools by their parents' decision. Because we came there for different reasons, the freshman class of the high school I attended represented for the first time in my experience a cross section of religious belief and practice. I have already described how carefully the teachers in that school sought to keep us in the church by presenting us with a religion that could survive our adolescent contempt for the sissified saintliness of grammar school. For a time they succeeded.

In that first year of high school we were not very aware of each other's religious positions, though it was clear that we had lost the enthusiastic uniformity of grammar school. Religion was not a favorite topic of discussion among boys, and there were no religious controversies to split us into factions. For the most part we listened passively to our instructors and rarely mentioned religion outside. When we left grammar school we had been liberated from the requirement that we attend religious services together, and since we lived in different parts of the city we had no way of knowing whether or not our classmates were observing the liturgical regulations of the Church. Nor did we care very much. High school held out the promise of new and exciting subjects of study; and religion, which had occupied much of our thinking in childhood, receded to a once-a-day-in-class, once-a-week-in-church experience. For the average student—who, again, is not our primary concern here—religion remained in that state until it assumed its comfortable and not very central niche in his adult life.

The better students soon regained their interest in religion, but only after it had been thoroughly transformed. Now the stress was theological, not liturgical. Our teachers made a great effort to present Catholicism as the most intellectually satisfying form of Christianity. We stopped studying religion and instead studied apologetics. Our idea of religion became a little earth-bound; instead of talking about devotion to God, we learned how to meet attacks on the faith with time-tested proofs of the reasonableness of Church doctrine. Apologetics had about it an air of gamesmanship. Even more than that, it was an eagerly received intellectual vindication of what we had previously accepted on faith. It served as a new support for holding *our* religion apart and above all others. Many of us—including both germinal liberals and conservatives—elevated apologetics to the position of a major religious concern.

High school was a time of rapid intellectual and emotional development. We were transformed in just a few years from children to young adults. As we passed the halfway mark, we began to assimilate more and more of our new knowledge into our religious framework and therefore broke down the rather narrow defensiveness that we had delighted in during the first few years. At first religion had been beset with enemies on all sides. As we studied further, religion became, perhaps too easily, an all-embracing view of the world able to reconcile all factions. Thinkers like Teilhard de Chardin encouraged us to think in terms of a synthesis of religion with other branches of learning. On our part, this longing for unity was partly a reaction to the increasing necessity of academic specialization on the one hand and the great proliferation of fields of study on the other. In any case, religion began to extend its reach, until some of us saw it as a key to history, personal psychology and even a philosophy of art.

This expansion of our idea of religion was initiated by what we knew of Catholic theology, but it soon outgrew that. Religion as apologetics was ideally suited to the rigidity and rationality of Catholic doctrine; religion as an explanation of history or art was not. That kind of talk was more intellectual gymnastics than religion, of course, but it speeded a change in our deeper sense of religion. For one thing, it led us to read in earnest, and our reading introduced us to Teilhard de Chardin who was instrumental in making us aware that all reality, including religion, was a process and not a static set of facts. That was perhaps the single most significant development in our religious lives. To pursue that concept it was necessary for us to reach outside our knowledge of Catholic theology, for example, to the Jewish tradition, which had always emphasized the eschatological and historical elements of doctrine. At this point "liberal" Catholic students began to split off from "conservative" ones, who, for the most part, chose not to go beyond apologetics. But the liberals were not at this point thinking of reforming Catholic doctrine or even of reforming the church. They were still operating in the realm of the intellect and still comfortable within their church.

Despite our pretensions of finding a religious philosophy that would answer all questions, there were a great many questions we were not asking at all. We were dealing for the most part with classical problems. I remember that we did a lot of talking about Christ as the archetypical tragic figure, and that sort of thing. We were dealing with concepts that much of our age, as we were to learn, had discarded as superficial; and we were failing to deal with the more fundamental questions that had already been raised. We were still thinking in terms of salvation, while much of the rest of the world was trying to find ways of making life bearable as an end in itself.

Our eyes were directed not at man, but at God, and we viewed man's groping for a life without Him with a pity that bordered on contempt.

When we were in our last year or so of high school, politics had begun to catch up with us. This was our liberal phase, however, and political liberalism fitted in nicely at first with our religious intellectualism. Students began at this point to make the first bridge between their theology and a social morality, but the first attempts were not very substantial or successful. It was easy to use Christianity to defend liberalism, or at least political humanitarianism, but this was often merely an attempt to prove once more that *our* religion had all the answers. Politics was just one area to which religion might be applied, and it was in this spirit that the social encyclicals of Pope John—especially *Mater et Magistra* and *Pacem in Terris* —were received. They were used by liberal students principally to argue with conservatives. There was no widespread feeling that the church should get involved in "political" questions. Most hoped, of course, that it might have something to say about racism and perhaps about nuclear warfare, but the built-in American suspicion of mixing religion with politics still held. The church was not expected to propose a detailed political program for the world but merely to work for clearly humanitarian goals such as peace and justice.

The major religious event of this period was the Second Vatican Council, but it is doubtful whether the Council had much effect on the spirituality of young people. The reforms introduced by the Council were mainly institutional, although such reform often involved re-statements of doctrine. The more obvious effects of the way in which the Council was conducted have already been noted. It demonstrated that the church was divided on many issues. We had imagined it to be monolithic in its unanimity. For the first time, the church was seen to be a changing society, subject to the same or similar laws of change as any society. Our wandering minds had become uncomfortable in the strait-jacket of Catholic doctrine, and the Council seemed to hold out the hope that doctrine might be liberalized. This hope preserved the loyalty to the church of many students who might otherwise have begun to stray.

As the devotional religion of our childhood was transformed into the more theological religion of late adolescence, a new element asserted itself—we discovered morality. I believe that discovery to be the key to the religion of my generation, for Catholics and non-Catholics alike. Theology, once discovered, subordinated spirituality to itself; morality, once undertaken as a personal consideration, submerged both. In the first shift, institutional religion was strengthened; in the second, it was virtually ignored. The roots of this discovery were both personal and public: we lost our old sense of morality when we encountered sex and evolved a new one as we became immersed in politics.

Morality had not been foremost in our minds in grammar school simply because living a life of sin did not seem an easy thing to do. The commandments to which we were bound took two forms, the decalogue and the religious requirements of the church. The former were self-justifying, and we could hardly imagine ourselves breaking them without a sense of guilt; the latter were justified in terms of the necessity of religious discipline, which we could at least appreciate. When we reached high school, however, we were introduced to sexual ethics, which were different from the other two. Sexual taboos were not self-justifying; in fact, they were imposed despite a certain amount of reluctance. Whether we kept the new rules or broke them, we were forced to ask ourselves what morality was built upon. Students had been able to ignore good morals before because they had been so easy; now we could not ignore them because their attainment had become so difficult.

The morality of grammar school had been based on a view of man that we understood and could accept. Sexual morality, on the other hand, did not seem to derive from a clear idea of either man or sexuality. The teachings of Jesus had a consistency, if only because, as we thought, they could be reduced to the golden rule. But the sexual ethic that was taught was almost mechanical—since everything depended on whether or not one was married—and this did not seem to have anything to do with any moral rule, golden or otherwise. This conflict will be considered more closely in chapter six, but we left high school with an unsettled view of how morality was *discoverable*.

Sexuality raised that question, and soon we found our increasing activity in politics providing an answer to it. The first revelation grew out of the civil rights movement. Students who went to the South, and even those who stayed home, were faced with racial hatred. This was a kind of sin they had not heard much about. The morality of grammar school, and even of high school, had been personal not social. It was based on individual responsibility for particular moral acts. There was very little notion that groups could be responsible for conditions which they could prevent. Sins of omission had been talked about, but the idea had never been applied to social responsibility. Moreover, there was a certain glibness in the morality we were taught. It was a standard quip of our high school teachers that "You have to love your neighbor, but you don't have to like him." What this meant in effect was that as long as we "loved" black people—in some abstract but actually meaningless sense—we did not have to *like* having them around. That meant that it was perfectly moral to keep them from finding a place to live in our neighborhoods.

The second revelation was that the Church was failing to instill in her members a strong sense of this "social" morality. Catholic activists who were spending most of their time arguing with other Catholics about race hatred wondered what the point of all their theological training had been if it did not instill a vigorous moral sensibility. Perhaps it was not fair to blame the church for the political conservatism of her members, but the students could not help wondering whether there had been some misplacement of emphasis in their Christian education. Because of their identification with the outcast black community, these young people read the Gospel teaching on the necessity of aiding the downtrodden with a new insight: Christ said time and time again that his followers would be recognized by their love for their fellow men. The whole complex structure of liturgy and doctrine had failed to bring most Catholics to this simplest appreciation of Christianity. Many activists asked themselves, therefore, if being Christian had any necessary connection with church structure. Did it not consist, rather, of loving in some special way? Did it not consist, that is, in *doing?*

Students who reached this point of perception came to college with a feeling that their moral sense was radically different from that of most of their fellow students. The Council had convinced them that the church was changing institutionally, but their contact with the enormous bigotry of too many Catholics convinced them that the problem of renewal was more complicated than the question of which language to use at Mass. Liberal Catholic students began to form a distinct faction on campus and in the Church. At first they did not feel at odds with the Church herself. They wanted to alter the emphasis of theological training, not discard it altogether. In fact, it was the liberal students who were the most devout and the most interested in the state of religion; it was liberals who pressed for improvement in the theology curriculum, and who gradually took control of the religious clubs on campus.

At college our study of theology really broadened. This was due partly to the improvement of the theology curriculum, but most seriously interested students had to do a substantial amount of the work on their own. Our excessive preoccupation with very abstract theology in the later years of high school cured many of us of that kind of speculation forever. Our increasing political awareness turned our theological interest more and more towards history and to theologies that emphasized the role of social change as a witness to the presence of God. We were also concerned at last with the great revolution that religion was undergoing in the twentieth century world. The "death of God" theology, whatever its merits, indicated by its very existence how troubled men were about their relationship to God. Catholic theology, it seemed, went right on replacing old speculations with new ones without dealing with what was happening to the faith of real people. We turned away from Catholic theology for the most part because most of what interested us was being written by non-Catholics.

The dominant theological influences were decidedly not abstract. We read Martin Buber, Archbishop Robinson, Bishop Pike and Harvey Cox. Our preoccupation was with conduct, not ideas. This was not really anti-intellectual, except to the extent that it opposed the detached intellectualism of our recent past; it was more a reaction against the tendency of theology to hopelessly ensnare itself in debate. Perhaps it was an

over-reaction. The fact remains that only the activists among
Catholic students were studying the whole range of contemporary theology with any seriousness at all.

Catholic doctrine did not survive that study very well because it was rigidly formulated. Our study emphasized process
and change. Students stopped thinking about many things
Rome considered important and turned to things she largely
ignored. The significant shift was away from the emphasis on
salvation that had characterized all our earlier religion. Life
after death was no longer discussed seriously. There seemed to
be no way of discovering anything about it. At any rate the
attainment of eternal life seemed a dubious motive for being
decent and responsible on earth. After all, "He who would
save his life will lose it." The longing for personal salvation
was replaced by a resolution to work for the fulfillment of
God's plan for history, whatever that might be. Religion in
grammar school had depicted life as a great game in which we
won or lost a place in heaven. The replacement of this very
negative view of life on earth with a new interest in human
history turned the eyes of students away from heaven and
towards man.

At the same time, students remained zealous for institutional reform of the church, even though their relationship
with the institution was slight. The few times students and
hierarchy did take note of each other's existence was when
friction developed between them. For all their zeal, there was
no way that young people *could* change the structure of the
Church. That was up to the hierarchy and with Paul VI in the
papacy the change that did occur seemed half-hearted and
insignificant. Things were happening, though, in small pockets
of the church allied with the political movement. This fact,
and the remarkable regeneration of the Church in Holland

and elsewhere, encouraged activist students to stick with the church no matter how estranged they had become from traditional formulations of doctrine. This lingering institutional concern was largely political and secular in the sense that students were concerned with making the church more tolerable as a human institution, that is, less authoritarian and more responsive to the real needs of her members. Their deeper religious life had worked itself free from the structure of the institution. Religion practiced by small groups of young people existed alongside and free of "the Church." When the existence of these groups began to embarrass the hierarchy, it took steps to suppress them. The history of one such case will show what the results were.

In the fall of 1965 a number of Catholic students and clergymen began active protest against the war in Vietnam. The efforts of the priests were spearheaded by the Clergy Concerned About Vietnam Committee, an interfaith group composed of both clergy and laymen that had been formed shortly before. In mid-November, Daniel Berrigan, the Jesuit priest-poet, was suddenly ordered to make a trip to Latin America in his role as an associate editor of the magazine, *Jesuit Missions*. At the same time, Daniel Kilfoyle and Frank Keating, two Jesuit priests who lived at St. Peter's College in Jersey City, were ordered to end their active association with the Clergy Concerned group. Father Berrigan's orders came from his superior at *Jesuit Missions;* Fathers Kilfoyle and Keating received their order from the Provincial Superior of the Order in New York. All three priests were given strong grounds to believe that the directives were issued at the urging of the New York Chancery Office, the headquarters of Cardinal Spellman's archdiocese.

Father Kilfoyle had for some time been presiding over a group of student activists who met weekly at St. Peter's for liturgy and a discussion, and Father Keating had often attended the meetings. The group was composed of politically active young people, and the orders to the priests discouraged them from participating. I had been a member of the group since the previous summer, and we were close and loyal to each other; yet we decided that for the moment there was not much we could do. A number of students at Fordham, however, none of whom were associated with the group, and many of whom did not oppose the policy of our government in Vietnam, decided that some kind of protest should be made about the political silencing of the priests. The movement began, strangely enough, in the Sodality—the traditionally submissive and other-worldly religious club on campus—and was organized by its officers. At any rate, I became involved in organizing the protest since I knew all the priests involved.

We decided to picket the residence of the Provincial on the Fordham campus and the Chancery Office behind New York's St. Patrick's Cathedral. The last decision turned out to be momentous because our demonstration was reported on the first page of the *New York Times,* was covered in all the other New York papers, was the subject of an editorial in the *New York Post,* and received coverage on television—all the things, in fact, to which a demonstration aspires. Apparently the affair was embarrassing to the Chancery—no one could recall such a demonstration having taken place before—and although the New York Archdiocese denied any role in the suppression of the priests, the restrictions on their activity were soon lifted. The demonstration also led indirectly to the writing of this book. It was on the picket line that I met John Leo, who was at that time an editor of *Commonweal,* and it was he who suggested that I be invited to the symposium which led to this book.

What kind of dispute had we engaged in? In one sense, it

was simply a political one: we might have been Czech students demonstrating against the silencing of a few intellectuals by the government. In another sense, the battle was religious and even theological: to what extent did a bishop or a religious superior have power to control the expression of priests on a question of morality, especially when the priests were attempting to apply the teachings of the church to a concrete situation to which their superiors dared not apply them? In fact, though, the question in our minds was simply one of power, of the relationship of the institution to the individual. We might have found the action of the institutional authority in this case particularly reprehensible, since they were authorities in a Christian church; but we might have protested a similar action by any institution. The behavior of church authorities in situations like this led to such a dilution of their religious influence that we were eventually content to ignore them altogether. As far as I know, this was the last attempt to silence priests in this manner in the New York Archdiocese. Since then contact between activist students and the Chancery has been negligible.

By this time politics began to take up more and more of the time of the very involved students, and this left less and less time for collective religious activity. Many Catholic students involved themselves in "underground" groups that revolved around a weekly liturgy, but religion was more and more pushed into that one corner of their lives. After the close of Vatican II the church seemed to move along at the same old sluggish pace, and institutional issues that had once seemed of great moment to young people now appeared to be parochial and frivolous in the light of the pressing domestic and international crises. Increasingly, then, Catholic student activists became merely student activists, as their energies were channeled completely into political and social work.

Yet it would be a serious misunderstanding to say that politics simply replaced religion, although that may seem to be what I have been implying. In fact, what we have called "politics" and "religion" have been replaced by something else. Once again I will call it personalism. Caught in simultaneous battles with their schools, their churches, and their government, young people realized that a similar kind of problem was at the root of all these battles. They were fighting for the right of self-determination in the most personal sense. They saw the modern world made up of super-powers and super-institutions that threatened from all sides the free development of individuals. Again, the problem was one of the distribution of power. Student activists wished to strip institutions of their power to manipulate persons, to treat them as a mass, rather than as individuals. In the midst of this effort the lines of demarcation between the different battles blurred so that it became impossible to say that, for example, our battle with the Chancery had been a "religious" dispute. Not only the students were subject to this. After all, the Chancery issue had grown out of the position of certain members of the hierarchy on the war in Vietnam.

The students' conception of the Chancery as an ordinary human, rather than religious, institution was the culmination of a gradual change in their idea of how religion and church structure were related. In grammar school, religion was wholly institutional and "the church" was the hierarchy. In high school, students conceived a much more active role for the laity. In college, the idea broadened again until "the church" meant *all* Christians. In that era of the Council and the first excitement of ecumenism, students still thought of religion in institutional terms but imagined that the institution would eventually encompass all Christian denominations. The political revolution, however, and the upsurge of moral emphasis which it induced, worked a final cleavage between religion and the institutional idea itself. Battles with bishops led many to believe that it was simpler not to deal with the hierarchy at all, to the diminution of student concern for institutional reform and to a loss of any concern for the institution at all.

One of the casualties of this falling away from the institution has been the interest of these students in theology. The very speculative idea of theology cultivated in high school gave way to a more down-to-earth "secular" theology later on. Most of this was written by liberal Protestants, but recently a good many Catholic theologians have begun to deal with the questions which concerned religious student activists. It is my impression, however, that most of these students have now lost their interest in theology altogether. Students have not stopped asking themselves "religious" questions, but they have grown suspicious of formal, institutional religion and therefore of formal answers to their questions. Even though theologians of all kinds are now probing the religious value of social reform, and even though some agree with students who contend that such labor can amount to religious practice (some would go so far as to elevate it to the level of the best kind of religious practice), young people seem no longer interested in their efforts. They consider it an act of appropriation for a theologian to try to place a stamp of religious validity on conduct they found valid on their own with precious little encouragement from the church.

Many young people not only do not want to formulate theological solutions to their problems, some of them find it dishonest of theologians to try to concoct theological solutions to what they see as institutional religious problems as well. A good example is the controversy that arose after the promulgation of Pope Paul's encyclical on birth control. Most theologians who opposed the teaching of the encyclical suggested that further theological discussion was necessary to refine the concept of the magisterium, the church's teaching authority. To many young people, equally opposed to the encyclical's teaching, this seemed an attempt to dress up in religious terms what was really an ordinary institutional problem. Students could not remember having been taught about anything in revelation that related very clearly to either birth control or to the composition of the magisterium. When theologians spoke of those things, they seemed merely to be couching their own notion of what was appropriate in theological terms. In effect, the students thought, each side was trying to claim God's stamp for its own idea of how conception should be regulated or how decisions should be arrived at by the Church.

The merits of the encyclical do not concern us here, since they will in chapter six; but the reaction of these students to the theological controversy is interesting. They saw these liberal theologians as men who felt that the pope's decision was not made in a proper manner. Specifically, they seemed to feel that they had not been sufficiently consulted, that is, that the decision was arbitrary; and that arbitrary decisions should not be made in the church. To a student activist this argument is very familiar. Students continually try to point out how many decisions which affect their lives are made without any participation on their part. This is one of the principal arguments against the draft and a major source of friction with university administrators. It might seem to the veterans of such frictions that while the theologians were really chafing under the quite ordinary belief that in a voluntary society momentous decisions should not be made without due concern for the collective opinion of the members, they found it necessary to discuss theological refinements in the concept of the magisterium. Activists did not expect that revelation would throw

much light on the subject; and since most of the tradition of
the church runs counter, they imagined that all this could
mean was that theologians would like to have an opportunity
to devise a more humane and responsible means of decision-
making within the church.

The students suspected that once such a scheme was de-
vised, arguments would carefully be drawn showing that this
was really the teaching of the church all along. This is rem-
iniscent of the practice of totalitarian countries who re-write
history to reflect the current idea of what it should be. Not that
students thought the theologians were hypocrites, but they saw
them as too often determined to prove that everything was
really known all along, even if only in germinal form. The
students saw no reason to go further than to admit that the
pope's decision was arrived at in a manner unacceptable to
free and intelligent men, that arbitrary decisions would not be
obeyed and that attempting to keep the bulk of the church's
members in a state of powerlessness and subjection was simply
self-destructive.

This does not indicate that student activists have become
non-religious, but merely that they are non-theological. Their
own version of personalist religion developed in their encounter with each other and in opposition to the many forms
of dehumanization which surround us. After a predominantly
conceptual education, against which they rebelled, they met
this new experience existentially. Activists are distrustful of
language despite its necessity. The rhetoric of their education
drained the meaning from words like "depersonalization,"
"prejudice," and "the poor." Students' discovery of the reality
behind these catchwords formed the foundation of their politics and religion. In order to preserve this reality in religion,
they turned against theological tradition, which seemed to ig-

nore it, and theological speculation, which seems too detached. Since their starting point is their own experience, they are more interested in exploring its ramifications than in discovering the relation of their experience to a theological tradition which they do not find nourishing.

For some students a kind of turning away from theology had begun even before their activism, when they discovered Jesus in high school. Catholics are considerably insulated from the Gospel, not because they do not know it, as some have suspected, but because they know a few parts of it too well. Those portions which are read at Sunday Mass become so familiar that they lose much of their impact. When we first read the Gospel all the way through as students, many of us found ourselves strongly drawn to the figure of Jesus and inspired by his message. For some this was a vital part of their liberal political phase, and they attempted to make direct applications of the Gospel to political problems—especially to the great human crises of war, poverty and racism. This was not an intellectual process but an existential one. They did not, for example, argue "just war theory," but asked instead whether Jesus could be conceived participating in any war. Their Christianity was a literal acceptance of Jesus' teaching.

Somewhere this closeness to Jesus seems to have been lost by most of these same students, although that phase of their evolution left lasting effects. Once more, politics was profoundly instrumental. When they reached the point of actually engaging in political activity, they found it necessary to communicate with others who had not undergone such an experience. Thus while most of our early arguments against the war in Vietnam stressed its immorality, it became increasingly necessary to stress its political and military impracticability as well, in order not to be dismissed as a Pacifist. The immorality of the war was never forgotten but came to be expressed more and more in ethical terms. This meant that Jesus as a person, even as Bonhoeffer's "man for others," receded somewhat, while his message remained, albeit with some intellectualization. Although his spirit may hover over the personalism of student activists, he has lost prominence in their religious discussion, even among believers. In the symposium described in the Foreword to this book, six students discussed religion for several hours, yet the only one who mentioned Jesus was a non-believer who said that Christ was "hip."

At the same time it is easy to see how compatible the personalism of the student activist—whether Christian, Jew, or agnostic—is with the teaching of the Gospel. When we were unsettled by the harsh traditional sexual code taught us in high school, we searched for a rationale out of which to squeeze all moral rules but without much success. Later, many decided that the moral precepts of the Gospel could be reduced to the maxim that all men are equal to all other men, that all men are to be treated as persons, not as things, or classes, or races —that is, not as Samaritans, or sinners, or poor men. What can be the meaning of the Gospel emphasis on helping the needy, if not that such aid asserts the equality of men despite their social condition? The Gospel ethic squares with the notion that religion is not belief, or membership but conduct that expresses a consciousness of the value of other persons. Religious men are to be recognizable by their love for one another. If this be so, then those young people who strive so fervently to appreciate the person in everyone, who fight so hard the universal tendency to reduce men to race, or faction, are as truly religious as any group the churches have produced.

This does not mean, of course, that all the students who got involved in politics are dropping out of the church like flies, into some huge amorphous body of secular humanitarians. There are probably not many left, though, whose theology could pass muster before the Roman Curia. In fact, I think I do not know a single activist student who is still conscious of himself as a Catholic, who has not adopted a theology that makes using the denominational label almost meaningless. Some students have lost interest in religion as an explanation of things separate from other explanations. A great many more feel strong ties to their religious tradition, but find the denominationalism of Christianity silly and try not to speak of themselves in such terms. Of course, we are discussing a process, and there are many young people now at different stages of the development that has been outlined. There is no guarantee that they will all reach the same conclusion.

As more and more activist students are sifted through this process, however, it becomes more possible to generalize about where they are heading. Observation would indicate that two basic groups are being formed. The first still identify with the institutional church to some extent, participate in group religious activity and maintain their interest in institutional reform. These students are generally personalists, and their religion is Jesus-oriented, although their conceptions of his significance vary widely. It is they who well might form the avant garde of the church's liberal wing in the future. The other group has broken all institutional ties and has generally given up the corporate practice of religion. For many of these, personalism is now both politics and religion, and they hesitate to define their religion just as they are reluctant to label themselves politically. This second group warrants closer examination. Previously, young people either stayed in the Church or left it; and, if they left, it was not to be "more religious" but

less—unless the defector joined another denomination. Now
we confront a large and growing group of young people who
have stopped calling themselves Catholic or even Christian;
who do not claim to have abandoned religion and yet hope to
found no church.

The group is diverse and not really self-consciously a group
at all, but certain generalizations can be made about the place
of religion in such students' lives. One obvious quality of this
religion is that it is not salvation-oriented. As long as religion
centered on the quest for heaven, Christians had been able to
hold themselves above the agony of their own century. But
when they tore their eyes away from heaven and looked instead at man, the whole thrust of their religious activity was
diverted. The view became not simply a "social Gospel" that
social reform was religion; rather, they saw religion as a rec-
ognition of something about man that led to a certain kind of
morality. Vertical aspirations are still very much in evidence,
but these aspirations are concerned with the transcendence of
man and not particularly with the existence of God. Personalism's religious character lies in its reverence, response, and
invitation to transcend even personality, and as such it is
rooted deeply in man—and faith.

Many of these activists of religious background have lost
their grasp on God, if only because they have lost contact with
prayer and religious practice and now concentrate on conduct. Even some who admit that they have no clear idea of
who or what God is, however, see their personalism as a form
of theism in which God remains a murky figure to be discovered only through continued dealings with men.

Whether they accept the view of Teilhard de Chardin who
sees the end of these efforts as a flowering of man's collective
consciousness or the view of someone like Harvey Cox who

thinks that we are creating God in history, personalism appears to be a potentially strong motive force in religious development. Teilhard says that universal love will draw evolution forward. Yet without the personalist content the idea of universal love seems a hollow abstraction. Cox says that every assertion of man's humanity—in fact, his love—is also an assertion of divinity. We are created in the image of God, and we make God possible by living as persons, not as animals or mechanisms. In either view personalism can drive history forward toward the end that God intends for it. In the view of these young people, God is not dead, but he will be if they do not prevent the world from being turned into an automated ant-heap. God will never die as long as persons live, for every loving act of theirs makes his existence possible.

For the student activists, religion of any kind cannot be preserved if man is allowed to be dehumanized. The churches have failed to perceive and address themselves to this critical problem of our age, and many students have chosen to live the life of their religion outside of churches. Their religion centers around the transcendence of man—the dimension that makes men equal despite their manifest inequalities—either as evidence of the presence of God, or as evidence only of the mystery of man. Slavery of almost any kind can destroy consciousness of that dimension, whether it be slavery to power, or to hatred, or to money or to mechanization. The thrust of this new religious emphasis is that man must be freed before any religion can flourish. To the extent that institutionalized religion has abdicated its role in the battle for this freedom to participants in the new religious vision, all religion depends for its future upon the activists' success.

5

the sectarianism
of the movement

I have discussed the educational, political and religious conflicts of young people as particular aspects of a single conflict between persons and institutions. These conflicts—whether with the university, the government or the church—most often engaged organized groups, not individuals. The nature of some of these groups will concern us here. We have been dealing with content, with certain events and ideas which have characterized the growth of student activism. To complete the picture, we must turn to form, to the groupings which transformed student activism from individual dissent to social movement. It is unnecessary to detail the history of the more prominent student political organizations. I prefer to single out two groups which I consider in some ways typical in order to determine what is implied for the content of activist student attitudes by the form of their organizations.

Some form of organization is imposed almost immediately as activist students begin to become distinct from the majority of their non-activist contemporaries. As a tiny minority they are likely to be segregated by the hostility of the majority and feel pressured to join a group for support. The taste for activism usually develops in students who already have a good deal in common and who band together politically and socially. For another thing, activist ideals normally develop in discussions outside the classroom. Since they are discovered by groups, it is natural to act upon them in groups. All these factors contribute to the formation of tight-knit "sects" of activists, which are both forums for discussion and focal points for action.

The qualities of these groups grow immediately out of the experience which led to their formation. Becoming an "activist" is not mere shifting of belief from one set of principles to another. Much more radically, it is the replacement of apathy by concern. Activism—whether for or against the status quo—means simply a commitment, a willingness to work either to preserve or to bring about an order of things deeply believed in. To become an activist is to be converted, with all the implications that the term suggests. The chief characteristic of activists is their fervor, not their goals. Many of the characteristics of activist groups speak more about fervor than ideology.

I would like to use as a model two groups which exemplify a number of these characteristics. One of the groups was religious, the other political. The first group met at St. Peter's College and has already been mentioned in connection with an attempted silencing of several priests associated with it.

The "Group" was formed in the spring of 1965 by a few activists who found themselves in a hostile religious environment and wanted a new channel of religious expression. The Group met once a week and celebrated a liturgy in what was then a very radical form: English was used throughout, and the form of the Mass was freely adapted. Almost all the participants were involved in some kind of political activity, and the group was therefore united on several levels. What bound it most strongly together was the shared experience of conversion to activism.

Since the average student views the university as his community, if religion is an important part of his life, it will naturally center there. For the activist, however, the problem is more complicated. Religious activists have undergone a conversion from the slumber of mechanical practice to a vital faith. Such students find themselves unlike their fellows at whom campus religion is aimed. On Catholic and non-sectarian campuses the church has failed to provide an adequate channel for their fervor, which is inclined to be critical of the mediocrity of most of what passes for student religion. As a result activists band together in *sects* where fervor is the rule, not the exception.

Clearly, worship in such a group will differ from a conventional church. All the forms of religious expression in the Group involved full participation. The number of those involved was small enough that a circle could be formed around the altar, everyone standing close enough to see everyone else. Since most participants knew each other well, there was an intimacy in the liturgy generally lacking in the services of large churches. A heightened awareness resulted directly from the participants' intense interest and their consciousness of themselves as actively involved.

Membership in the Group was always in a state of flux. It had begun with a small number of close friends who composed its nucleus for several years, but each week there were also new participants. Sometimes these stayed and joined the regular participants, and sometimes they left after attending a meeting or two. At the same time, students who had been with the Group since its formation were occasionally separated from it as they changed schools or changed their religious ideas. The Group was simultaneously always reaching out and touching new lives and losing its hold on others who had learned from it all they cared to. As such, it was a kind of microcosm of the "movement" at large.

Fervor led the Group to a strong conviction that they were in many ways the authentic Christians in the church, and that the larger institution was off the track. It would be unwise to dismiss this elitism too simply. Activists like these were really concerned about religion, and most of the ostensibly Catholic students who surrounded them—and jeered at them—were obviously not. The opposition of more conventional Catholics produced a feeling of persecution that naturally heightened the Group's isolation and, therefore, its pride. Separation from the majority by a gulf of hostility proved to be an important feature of the Group's development.

Another quite different group which is a good illustration of the activist sect is the Student Peace Union. This was an organization unlike the New Left groups in some respects. The contrasts it presents with them will be illuminating. The Student Peace Union, "S.P.U.", was founded in the late 50's by a group of the first activists that my generation produced. These were students of varying political beliefs who became concerned about the threat of nuclear war and organized to work for its prevention. SPU was never a huge organization and most of today's students have probably never heard of it, but it did enjoy substantial success in the early 60's, when it attracted several thousand students in the first stages of political awareness. At the time, it was virtually the only broad-based student peace organization in the country. Several of the older Pacifist groups were working to recruit youth, but they had already developed fairly complete ideologies. SPU, on the contrary, was open to members of any political stripe, as long as they wished to work for peace.

When I joined SPU in the summer of 1965, both its membership and executive committees were politically very mixed. The steering committee, for example, included a Republican Pacifist who worked on Wall Street, a Democratic Socialist, a Jesuit seminarian, a "World Federalist," and a few garden variety liberals. This diversity was a source of the organization's appeal. It made it possible for us to speak to a large number of students convincingly by showing that activity for peace need not be "Pacifist," or "Leftist." The failure of SPU to accept a single political ideology led eventually to its destruction, but during the first year of my membership it enjoyed increasing influence among the growing body of students who were drifting away from the civil rights movement. Many of these were Catholic students who wished to work for peace, but who did not wish to associate with any group that was considered "leftist."

Almost all of SPU's earlier efforts were directed towards students. SPU, like most student organizations, was composed of largely autonomous chapters with their activities focused on their own campus. The typical chapter sponsored discussions, invited speakers and distributed peace literature to students. Direct action, such as demonstrating, was usually on a small scale at that time and was usually aimed at very specific goals.

When demonstrations were conducted, statements explaining their purpose were handed out to onlookers. In the New York headquarters, the steering committee produced statements on issues which involved threats to peace and circulated them among students and government officials. The whole emphasis was upon communication. Young people who had lost their faith in the brinksmanship of the Cold War tried to explain its folly to others.

There were, of course, obvious contrasts and similarities between these two activist sects—the Group and SPU—but the membership of the two groups frequently overlapped. Those who were connected with both often thought of them as two expressions of the same movement. At the same time, the two groups served clearly different functions. This is why they managed to exist side by side. SPU aimed at conversion, while the Group was concerned with its own members. Anyone who wanted to come was welcome, but there was no advertising, and indeed, there was a fear that if the Group grew too large it would lose its vital intimacy. We might say that SPU was the public, political expression of its members' activism, while the Group was a relatively private, religious expression of much the same spirit. The essential ingredient common to both—the fervor of the conversion to activism—structured their critique of the larger institutions which contained them and determined their fate.

The Group's principal criticism of the church, and its reason for being was the lack of fervor of most Catholics. The members of the Group were converts. At some point in their high school or college education they had been converted to their religion, while most other students either ignored it or took it for granted. They saw that most of the members of the church were not vitally concerned with the moral demands of religion. They had not really chosen the church but had been born into it. This seemed to the members of the Group to be the reason for the apathy of so many Catholics but also of the dominance of the clergy.

The church seemed overly preoccupied with maintaining its membership level, an effort that resulted from the traditional emphasis on salvation as a reward for visible participation in the church. The clerical hierarchy emphasized those aspects of religion, especially the dogmatic and disciplinary, which would hold the membership together. At the same time, as the institutional church adjusted itself to the various societies in which it found itself, it became difficult for it to criticize society or to demand conduct of its members which might conflict with social customs. In fact, the church seemed unwilling to make any rigid moral requirements of its members, except for sexual ethics. Not that the church was totally uncritical of society, but its attacks on materialism, pleasure seeking and the "vices" of modern society were rarely aimed very clearly. Efforts to mobilize the church membership on certain issues— such as the threats of Communism, or pornography—always seemed to be campaigns that would be approved by the more conservative elements of society. It remained unthinkable that the American churches might, for example, condemn militarism or unfair business methods.

The church, as manifested in the religious life of the parish, disappointed the young and led to the formation of groups like the one at St. Peter's. Parish religion, aimed at the common denominator of the community, does not move many beyond that level. If this does not destroy the faith of young people— and it sometimes does—it certainly weakens their confidence in its institutional expression. Parish religion is not empty for everyone, of course, but it is rigid and rarely provides any outlet for the fervent religious energy of the young. For students, once again, it is not so much "liberalism" as it is religious fervor that determines the nature of dissent.

Political activism has its own causes, as we have seen; but here, too, fervor plays a leading role. The students who detached themselves from the Cold War mania felt that the rest of the nation was sound asleep to political realities. The ideology of the government plays a role similar to the dogma of the church. Consensus and unity come to be valued over free discussion and "law and order" over individual liberty. Activists are separated from this consensus by the very fact that they are active. Their attempts to examine political realities critically, whatever their success, set them apart from the majority of their fellow citizens. The political system offers little hope of change to young people because mobilizing the huge apathetic mass of the population seems impossible. After what they consider President Johnson's betrayal of the electorate on the Vietnam issue, students became reluctant to work for the election of liberals, whose promises, they felt, could not be believed.

Student activists are often accused of advocating the destruction of American society, but when they first began their disaffection from it they clearly thought that they were working for its preservation. The first encounters with racism and the Vietnam War made many young people think that America had strayed from its course, but that these problems were temporary blights in an otherwise free and healthy society. More serious and prolonged involvement with these problems, and especially the later discovery of the true dimensions of racism in America, led to the estrangement of some students from what they regard as an essentially corrupt society. However, whether the goal of the students is modification or transformation of our national life, most activists would agree that their efforts are directed towards the conventional American ideals of liberty and equality of opportunity. On both the religious and political scene, students find themselves more dedicated to what they regard as the true ideals of state and church than the bulk of the population. At the same time, both groups find that there are no adequate channels to implement their fervent vision of a new world. Both groups of students form organizations which reflect the intense concern they find lacking in society.

How do these groups answer, in their form of organization and their programs, the criticisms of the student activists who created them? The features of the groups are direct responses to the flaws seen in the Church. The fact that membership was based on dedication to common aims determined all the other characteristics of the Group I belonged to. It was non-hierarchical. Priests led the Group only in the liturgy, and they became members by a natural selection on the part of the other participants. The Group was non-dogmatic even to the extent that several non-Catholic Christians became regular members. At the same time, of course, the Group enjoyed a remarkable unanimity in its concerns. But the unanimity was not forced since only those who felt comfortable in the Group's atmosphere bothered to attend regularly. To underline a distinction already drawn several times, there was a wide divergence of belief but much less variance in the participants' norms of conduct. This was an exact reversal of the situation in the church at large.

The case of the Student Peace Union is somewhat different. SPU saw itself not as an organizational model for a changed political structure but as an ideological model. The groups of the New Left, on the other hand, have come to see themselves

as primarily political. While earlier groups like SPU try to
influence the existing structure, newer ones want a measure of
control over it. In their internal workings they seek to demonstrate the participatory democracy they hope to see realized in
the nation as a whole.

Because both of these groups have dissolved, I have used
them instead of the burgeoning New Left as examples of
stages in the development of the student activist movement.
Their failure indicates where the movement is headed, how it
is changing and what problems it must cope with to survive.

The Group died of monotony. During the three years of its
existence it became inbred. The core of participants came to
know each other so well that discussion became less and less
interesting. New participants were usually less advanced than
the regulars, and so they failed to infuse new life into the
meetings. Dissent was never suppressed, but it slowly drowned
in a sea of consensus. Without conflict, discussion became
even more dull. The Group became cut off from the institution
at large. It soon became the only religious activity of many of
its members who cared little about bickering with or about
bishops, once they learned how easy it was to ignore them.
When participants drifted away from the Group—as they did
when they changed schools, graduated, or lost interest—they
more often than not drifted away from community worship
altogether. Religious organizations like the Group are quite
common on campuses now, and all may not dissolve in this
fashion, but the flaws in the structure of the Group may also be
weaknesses in many of its counterparts.

This does not mean that communal worship is dispensable,
although it was dispensed with when the Group dispersed. The
needs that liturgy answers remain, but new forms are beginning to be found. A kind of liturgical emphasis has marked

the activist political movement, for example. In the early civil rights struggle with its strong religious accent there were many gatherings especially in the South that approximated religious celebrations. More recently I attended a meeting in the chapel at Yale for a ceremony to mark the turning-in of a number of draft cards. The service included breaking of bread and a common meal, but most of the participants regarded it as a "secular" service. Because liturgy is, among other things, a celebration of the apartness and shared fervor of a community, we can expect that activist groups, whether specifically religious or not, will continue to evolve forms of group ritual, which approximate and may replace for many young people the traditional religious liturgy.

SPU died from both external and internal pressure. The external pressure was the sharp rise of the student New Left in the mid-60's. SPU was concerned mainly with peace, while SDS (Students for a Democratic Society) appealed to activists who wished to fight for reform on several different fronts under the same organizational banner. SDS was also more appropriate for the growing number of students who felt that the problems of race, poverty and peace were related to more fundamental flaws in American society and should not be treated as separate issues. SPU's membership fell off as SDS grew rapidly. It was mainly the influx of Catholic students, who were slower in becoming activists because their backgrounds were extremely conservative, that kept SPU from dying at once.

The internal pressure came from younger members whose militancy worked against SPU's traditional political pluralism. These were students with experience in several kinds of political activism and they found themselves in broad agreement on many points of ideology and tactics. They wanted the orga-

nization to reflect this broader agreement. Before this time the
only thing that held the different factions together was their
common concern for peace. Since the earlier emphasis in SPU
had been on communicating with society at large, the political
diversity of the organization facilitated this task and assured
organizational literature of a wide appeal. As the membership
became more dogmatic, however, so did the organizational
literature, and statements began to be framed in a language
and tone that only the initiated could understand or be moved
by. Caught between the Scylla of dwindling membership and
funds, and the Charybdis of a rising militancy that threatened
to destroy the communication that was at the heart of SPU's
purpose, its governing board finally dissolved the organization.

Whether either of these groups is strictly typical or not,
their history indicates several things about religious and political activism among students and about the peculiar problems
of that activism. The strength of these sects—their intense
fervor—has an inherent weakness which leads to their separation from society. Once cut off, they often develop in ways
that render them unintelligible to nonmembers and therefore
reduce their ability to affect others. The original reason for
their formation may have elicited wider sympathy, but after a
time the organization speaks a language developed within itself and not geared to the preconceptions of those outside it.
Religious and political sects like these often form around a
battle for greater tolerance as individuals who wish to maintain their right to a minority viewpoint band together to defend it. But that defense, when it results in isolation, may
produce in the new sect an intolerance of the views of everyone else.

This is not an inevitable result, but the tension which underlies it is always present in activist groups. A clear example of this tension can be drawn from the experience of religious activists. Many such students began their battle with the institutional church by attacking her dogmatism, especially her moral dogma. These students, who adhered to one or another notion of situation ethics, stressed the necessity for freedom of conscience and tolerance of failure. They rejected the black-and-white moralism of their religious education and sought a more flexible approach that would allow for wide personal divergence in conduct. After their initiation into politics, however, these same students developed a sense of social responsibility which placed a serious duty on all individuals to act in a socially responsible manner. While they had become extremely tolerant of personal lapses from the church's sexual code of morals, for example, they now became extremely intolerant of lapses from their own code of social morals.

This somewhat parallels the development of political consciousness, of course. Students whose interest in politics was generated by an abhorrence of the Cold War intolerance of diverse political belief often find themselves after a few years of political activity to be as devoted to their new political ideology. The dehumanizing polarization of East and West has been replaced by a sometimes equally dehumanizing polarization of New Left and everyone else. One of the principal targets of activists has always been social manipulation, especially of poor people and minority groups. But once these activists have evolved a more complete picture of the society they would like to create, many of them do not hesitate to choose means to that end—such as violent confrontations which often involve manipulating people rather than changing them.

The elitism of the activist sect, then, is simultaneously

dangerous and the source of its vision. The dangers will be clearer if we consider the alternatives facing such a sect after a number of people join together to work for a common vision of how things should be. What can a sect like the Group do to promote its vision, taking for granted that change is produced through the exertion of power of some sort? The sect could try to influence those who hold power in the church to alter the institution's structure. If this failed, the sect probably could not seize power itself, since sectarianism of the activist sort does not lend itself to mass movement. What happens, therefore, is that sects that fail to satisfy themselves that they are influencing the larger institution tend to detach themselves more and more from it. Theoretically, such a group could go on existing forever, minding its business and ignoring the local church authorities; but young people will not be content with a vision which they cannot see accomplished. Once removed from a position of influence, such sects die of their own irrelevance just as the Group did.

The alternatives facing a political sect are similar. It can seek to influence those who already hold power by communicating to them the sect's insight into the flaws in the social structure. This has been the first phase of most of the political activism of this decade. The civil rights movement, for example, was initially aimed almost entirely at whites, who hold the power to effect a change in the status of blacks. The early student political groups, like SPU, were similarly engaged in efforts to speak to Americans who had not experienced liberation from the Cold War. Communication was the goal of all this activity and this goal shaped their rhetoric. Civil rights groups were conciliatory, not accusatorial; peace groups spoke to government officials and did not condemn them outright. Whether or not these attempts had much real effect, almost all activists decided fairly early that they were not enough.

Another alternative offered to the religious sects was to simply drop out of the institutional structure, but this alternative is not open to the political sect. Individuals, like Timothy Leary and the hippies, have tried to drop out with various degrees of success. Two factors, however, have made this an unattractive solution for most students deeply involved in politics. The first is their notion of social responsibility. The student revolution is not entirely self-directed; that is, while agitation does go on for student power, much student political activity is directed towards the enhancement of the power of others, such as blacks and the poor. To drop out might prevent a certain amount of personal frustration, but for most activists the frustration would be replaced by guilt. Moreover, it is not really possible to drop out of the nation (even by going to Canada) in the same way that one can ignore a religious institution because the power of the nation is unavoidable. The draft and taxes implicate young people in government policy whether they like it or not.

The third alternative is for the sect to secure power itself. A religious sect cannot do this because it cannot mount a mass movement among the apathetic. But in politics mass movement is not the only way of taking power. The civil rights movement was transformed from an attempt to gain sympathy from powerful whites, to an effort to secure power for blacks. We can now observe a similar transformation of the student political movement. Student organizations which began by trying to sway the opinion of policy-makers now are trying to gain enough power for themselves to make policy. A few hope to do this through violent revolution, which most Americans would dismiss as madness or subversion. (It should be remembered that this has become more common only because the dissent of such students has often been suppressed violently.)

Others place a certain limited faith in conventional political processes and hope to elect enough candidates of the "New Politics" to effect change through a peaceful shift of power. The defeat of Eugene McCarthy and the increasing polarization of the nation signalled by the victory of Richard Nixon and the strong showing by George Wallace guarantee that this method will take frustratingly long to produce results. A third group disavows both violence—except in retaliation—and elective politics and seeks rather to demonstrate the conviction that the political system is corrupt and undemocratic. It is difficult to envisage at this point how this process of confrontation will effect a change in the balance of political power nationally.

By its very nature, the sectarian vision will be unpopular in the sense that it will be uncommon. Young activists will always be hampered in their efforts at reform by the fact that most of the population does not share their conviction. If change is to come, it will probably be received by most people more passively than passionately. This means that change will continue to take place at the top, and not at the roots of society—community organizing among the poor and blacks is the exception. The danger is that activists will work to impose change upon the population in a manner that amounts to a substitution of new forms of manipulation for the old ones. Activists who are understandably frustrated over the unconcern of the unconverted often accept this solution as inevitable and as justified in the pursuit of a good goal.

Such a solution recalls the paradox of the religious student who is liberal in personal morals and strict in social morals. A political parallel centers around the difference between power over oneself and power over others. Political activism began among this student generation as an assertion of the right of persons to manage their own lives free from exploitation. But it became clear that liberation from exploitation required that power be exerted over the exploiters. In other words, the status of blacks could not be altered without a corresponding alteration in the circumstances of some whites, and students could not gain power without an adjustment in the power of university administrators, and so on. The paradox of the activist's passion is that he wishes to provide maximum freedom for the individual, but he knows that to secure freedom for all means abridging the freedom of some. If an activist group does not direct its passion toward others—that is, if it is content with its own freedom—it will die of irrelevance just as the group at St. Peter's did. If, on the other hand, it is so devoted to liberating others that it becomes so dogmatic that it is willing to sacrifice diversity in order to secure a concerted effort, it will become as depersonalizing as the forces it opposes. SPU might have become bogged down with dogmatism if it had not been spared by disbanding.

The balance between individual freedom and social responsibility can best be maintained if the movement retains its personalist underpinnings. Personalist politics revolves around the paradox that persons are both individuals and parts of a social whole. Young people who have rejected both individualism and Communism try continually to avoid the tendency to fall back into one of those oversimplifications. A humane political philosophy would be based on the double premise that all men must be free, and all men must be equal. No man must be exploited or manipulated, nor must any man in his freedom be allowed to manipulate others. The personalist would similarly resolve the religious conflict between individual freedom and social morality. In matters which concern one's power over oneself—the areas of freedom of belief and

primacy of conscience—the personalist will be a libertarian.
In matters that concern power over others—"social morality"
—he will be strict. To maintain with the personalist that one is
fulfilled through his relationships with others is to recognize
the inseparable importance of both the individual and social
dimensions of the person.

How can this approach benefit students who wish to change
their society? The activist movement has reached a watershed
of sorts now that political communication is replaced by confrontation, and religious students seem to have largely abandoned their attempts to reform religious institutions. Both of
these shifts communicate, but they signal the *end* of communication. The danger is that they aggravate the deadly polarization in the midst of which my generation was reared. Religious
activists who brush off conservative churchmen as "un-Chris-
tian", and activists who assume that all frightened Americans
are Fascist bigots are indulging the same black-and-whiteness
they were brought up on. Instead of reducing dehumanizing
factionalism, they have become the most factious group of all.
It would reform our society if power were shifted to the
powerless; but a radical change in our society will be accomplished only if the formerly powerful and the formerly powerless are reconciled. Any activist who does not in some way
appreciate the dilemma of his "enemies"—whether this may
be Pope Paul wrestling with the problem of birth control or a
white suburbanite terrified of black people—is not a revolutionary. He is merely a new manipulator who may happen to
be on the right side. A true revolution would free the slave
from his subjection and the master from his fear.

Activist students, separated from their fellow citizens as
they are by their very activism, are automatically turned into a
faction. The methods they choose to pursue their vision will

determine whether that natural gulf will be bridged or widened. Because their activism is a source of discomfort and fear for many of their countrymen, we can expect that the number of incidents of repression will increase and that many students will retaliate. Means will, of course, always corrupt ends. I fear not so much that students will become totalitarian —there is not much prospect of their achieving enough power to make that threat real—but that they will lose all concern for the defenders of the status quo. Then what began as a quest for reconciliation will end as the greatest division in this nation since the Civil War.

6

the sensibilities
of the movement

I do not want to give the impression that all of the distinctive behavior of my generation can be reduced to the conscious pursuit of "activist" ideals. Many of the most striking ways in which young people stand apart from their elders involve their life style, not their ideology—although the two are related. Both older and younger people expect the life style of the young to be somewhat disturbing, and this student generation has certainly fulfilled that expectation. But the fact that cultural revolt of the sort manifested in trends in music, dress and sexual conduct is normal and expected may too easily hide its significance. By such means, among others, young people demonstrate their unique view of things, when they are not doing so more explicitly. This chapter will explore some of the tensions we have been discussing as reflected in my generation's cultural milieu.

We are more in search of a mood here than of a philosophy. As far as I can tell, young Americans today are not accustomed to formulating their ideas in abstract philosophical terms. The positivist tradition which has dominated philosophical education in this country has made many students uncomfortable in the realm of metaphysics. We are not inclined to sit around and explicitly speculate about ultimate values. The increasing influence of behaviorism and behaviorist sociology has made students wary of "metaphysical" explanations of human conduct. Existentialism has, of course, been a counter force to this development, especially among activists; but it has influenced their ideas about conduct more than communicating notions about the nature or purpose of existence. This means that we must not look for a philosophy among students because they are largely unaware that they have any. We must seek out their mood in some of the ways they choose to express it.

Two facets of their mood will concern us here: sexuality, the manner in which young people relate to persons; and art, the style of their relation to the objects which surround them.

THE SEXUAL REVOLUTION

The sexual revolution—whatever we may decide it really is— has two kinds of importance for an understanding of the development of my generation. The first is completely straightforward: the revolution in sexual values and conduct forms a significant element of the chain of phenomena that sets my generation apart. The second is more illustrative: some of the themes that run through the sexual revolt lead to a deeper appreciation of the view of man under consideration by young people. What follows should be approached with this double significance in mind. This is not an attempt to explain what sexuality is, but it is an attempt to describe how certain changes in sexual ideas and conduct have helped to form my generation's ideas about relationships and conduct of every kind.

We must consider what youth is revolting against. Conventional sexual morality—if I can be permitted to disregard its complexity for the sake of generalization—has been strangely unselfconscious. It has not been the kind of ethic that grows gradually more complex as its implications are unravelled. Ordinary sexual morality has been incredibly simple, even simplistic, and it is not very prone to extending its grasp of reality. The ethic has only one tenet: people who are not married must not indulge in serious sexual activity. The form of this sanction says something about what sex is imagined to be but not very clearly. We gather at once, though, that sex and marriage are intimately connected, and we can begin to try to understand this ethic by speculating why this should be so.

Two reasons link sex and marriage in the conventional morality. They are the "pragmatic" and the "religious" reasons. The pragmatic view centers around the fear of unwanted pregnancy. Because of the danger of conception, it sees sex as potentially exploitative of women and, if unregulated, a threat to marriage. By marriage is meant the public commitment of people to rear together the children whom they conceive. The religious view is based upon one or another version of natural law. In its more traditional formulation, this view sees sex as primarily intended by God as an instrument of creation or, more simply, of procreation. Both views are heavily steeped in the social impulse towards the protection of women, and the discouragement of illegitimacy.

That prevention of socially undesirable pregnancies is close to the roots of each view explains in part the way in which they are inculcated in the young. At first it is possible for teachers to simply build an aura of danger and prohibition around the whole sexual domain. For early adolescents, sex is seen as wrong in the same way that "dirty" words are shocking. This first ethic cannot forever withstand the growing fascination of sex, however, and so the moral education of young people becomes more concrete as they grow older. In later adolescence the very practical fear of pregnancy is laid on over the older generalized fear of sex itself. The former remains, of course, and together the two kinds of fear are potent safeguards of sexual morality.

Now this fear of pregnancy is obviously less compelling as an argument for the chastity of boys, at least in terms of persuasiveness. For this and a variety of other reasons, the conventional sexual morality has concentrated on women. Men are pretty well left to act as they please. Of course they are not usually told that, but their sex education contains within it a kind of implicit gentlemen's agreement that men can indulge in sexual activity if they must, as long as they do not go about corrupting "nice girls." The effect of the double standard is that girls are supposed to bear the moral burden of their relationships with boys. Girls must draw the line in sexual conduct and boys, who have come to expect them to, are therefore freed from having to make any moral choices at all. Sex for men becomes by implication a matter of getting what satisfaction they can and for girls of giving as little as possible.

There has been deviation from conventional standards in every generation, of course, but that deviation has itself been almost conventional, and it is therefore not revolutionary. Whatever lapses an adult may have experienced in his youth, when it came time to educate his children, he insisted upon the ethic in unchanged form. The concern here is not with this kind of deviation but with changes in sexual conduct that have forced a change in young people's understanding of sexuality. These are the changes that may result in a different kind of education for the next generation.

Many reasons have been advanced for the revolution in sexual activity among the young. I am using the term "sexual revolution" to mean that more and more young people are engaging in serious sexual activity before marriage. But the principal factor in the breakdown of the old ethic is the improvement of contraceptive technique. The pill has undercut both the pragmatic and religious aspects of the traditional ethic. Pragmatically, the pill has severely reduced fear of pregnancy, and it has prevented the exploitation of women by insuring that they will not become pregnant. Realization that this breakthrough has damaged the basis for conventional morality has also affected the religious ethic. Many young people have come to see religious sexual morality as the pragmatic norm dressed in religious clothing. This somewhat resembles the discovery by the black poor of the extent to which "law and order" is designed merely to protect the status quo. What once was seen as a question of good and evil now seems merely a matter of social stability. In neither case does the revelation lead to complete disregard of the norm—to lawlessness or promiscuity—but the conviction that what was once thought sacred is really a matter of convenience has gone far towards destroying the old instinctive fear.

The pill has manifestly led to an increase of sexual activity among young people, but that is not in itself revolutionary, although this is what most people think of as the "sexual revolution." To be sure, the dimensions of the old ethic are being changed. The pill has made women equal to men in that it has

freed them from the heavy burden of having to choose between continence and possible pregnancy. Many young
women as a result seem to have joined men in a permissive
sexual morality based more on aesthetics and opportunity
than on ethics. This is not a repudiation of the old morality. It
is merely the logical extension of it. Since sexual prohibition
was based on fear of pregnancy, the elimination of fear has
eliminated the prohibition. Many parents have been made
painfully aware of the logic of this development by their inability to convince their children that they should not indulge
in sexual activity even if they are protected against pregnancy.

I should not like to give the impression that the new permissiveness is always as cold-blooded as this seems. In fact,
one of the earmarks of my generation has been its attempts to
find moral rationales for activity that its predecessors treated
more pragmatically. Politics is one example; sex is another.
Most conscientious young people have tried to develop standards for sexual conduct to replace the simplistic and universal prohibition of pre-marital sexual activity. The most
common standard they have evolved has been based on love
and respect, in which sexual activity is seen as permissible
between people who love each other and, (a frequent stipula-
tion) who plan to marry. Some such standard has been forced
on many young people by the increasing length of their education. Young couples who a generation ago might have married
after college are now required to accommodate themselves to
a waiting period that extends several years beyond. The most
common accommodation has been serious sexual activity
within a context of love and a commitment to eventual
marriage.

As far as I can tell, this kind of standard has not effectively
replaced conventional morality, even though it seems to have

worked for many couples. Frequently, couples who enter such a relationship eventually break up, and then have to adapt to the habit of intimacy which they have formed. This is very common among college girls. They become intimate with a boy friend whom they hope to marry, break up with him for some reason, then are intimate with someone else whom they like or love, but do not plan to marry. Finally, they are intimate with whomever they want in much the same fashion as men at college may be. This does not seem to me to indicate that the old standard should be returned to, however. On the contrary, parents who deplore promiscuity in their daughters ought to realize that it is a direct result of the old ethic and not a revolt against it.

The trouble with the conventional rule is that it provided no truly moral standard for sexual conduct but merely a mechanical rule. Nothing was permitted outside of marriage but everything within it. This rule-of-thumb gave young people no clear idea of what sexuality *is*—in fact, it had nothing to do with sexuality, but only with genital sex. The Catholic tradition of sexual morality makes explicit many of the presumptions of the conventional American sexual ethic, and so it can serve as a good illustration. In the Catholic scheme, sex was primarily intended for procreation. Not only was sex primarily biological, but primarily genital. Any idea of sex that did not fit into this scheme was deemed "unnatural." Contraception was condemned because it separated sex from procreation, thus destroying its natural purpose. It was admitted that sex could have other purposes, but these were usually described simply as "pleasure," which was vaguely frowned upon. To be perfectly honest sex meant copulation, which was looked upon as a dangerously pleasurable way of conceiving children.

This view might seem harmless, if somewhat limited, but its ramifications were often gruesome. My religious education, for example, provided no standards for the morality of sex within marriage. We were told of the "marriage right" and the "marriage debt", which were acquired at marriage by men and women, respectively—but not, it seemed, reciprocally. These legalisms meant that it was immoral for a wife to refuse her husband's advances, a view so mechanical as to be sickening. The traditional Catholic teaching on sex was immensely degrading to women. It reduced them to their child-bearing function and did not take into consideration their feelings or rights as persons. This ethic was enshrined as a protector of women because it insisted that men not impregnate women unless they married them first. As long as men committed themselves to the support of their wives and children, however, wives were to be sexual slaves. This is not just a lingering memory of a Victorian notion that was once more widely accepted. An examination of very recent developments—such as Pope Paul's encyclical on birth control written after "agonizing" reappraisal of the church's view of marriage—demonstrates that the church's position continues to be grounded in a wholly functional view of women and of sexuality.

This view of sexual morality demanded that women exercise complete restraint before marriage and allowed them very little restraint after it. The revolt against this ethic by my generation should have harmonized these poles by allowing women the privilege of restraint both before and after marriage. They should have been freed from sexual exploitation in either state but should also have been made to some extent sexually free in both. Again, I think that this has not happened universally. The earlier rule had let men run wild, and in many instances the new freedom has succeeded only in letting some girls join them. This is so because, although young people have largely rejected the simplistic conclusions of traditional morality, they have not risen above its premises. Sex is still seen as copulation, as a pleasurable means of conception. Since most young people believe that contraception is permissible, they see sex as merely pleasurable. The only choice left is that of a partner and the standards become more broad as time goes on.

Actually, the picture is not uniformly this bleak. Use of the pill *has* led to more widespread sexual permissiveness, but this is not really what the sexual revolution is all about. The real revolution in sexual morality is occurring among young people who have examined the traditional ethic and reject its premises as well as its mechanical conclusion. These students are veterans of the first revolt. They rejected the old morality as unpragmatic but have found that simple permissiveness is not enough. They watch their friends who vowed to be intimate only with those they loved become less and less selective and see that sex itself is once more being reduced to mere biology. Those who are concerned see that this is really just the old ethic plus the pill, and wonder whether there isn't a real moral standard to replace it.

The standards they are evolving seem to be related to the personalist consciousness that they developed in their encounter with politics. The key moment in the political history of my generation was the discovery of exploitation in all its subtle forms. Men have always been somewhat conscious of the evil of manifest exploitation like slavery, but the insight of this generation—of course, not exclusively theirs—has deepened to a conviction that we are all prone to depersonalization and manipulation. In some cases this insight has been applied to sexuality; in others it was derived from it. In both, the personalist emphasis separates those who have discovered it both from the old strictness and the new permissiveness.

Paradoxically, the personalist sexual ethic rejects the premises of conventional sexual morality, but preserves its conclusions by expanding them. The old morality was based wholly on biology, and thus treated women as mechanisms. In the traditional Catholic view, woman is more a receptacle for man's seed than a person. While rejecting this as dehumanizing, the personalist accepts and expands the conclusion of the old morality, which was based on a concern that women not be sexually exploited. It was felt that women would be protected if sex was confined to marriage where the man would have to support the fruits of it. The personalist sees a much more subtle exploitation from which both women and men have to be protected. In this view, any sexual activity is wrong in which a person is treated as an object, whether as a manufacturer of babies, a source of pleasure or some sort of a sedative.

Sexuality presents one of the most dangerous possibilities of exploitation open to persons in their everyday lives. There is no mode of expression in which one can so directly use another or in which selfishness is so widely permitted. Conversely, sexuality can be a perfect expression of the personalist paradox of individual fulfillment through relationship with others, since one of its fundamental elements is the attainment of satisfaction through its gift. When sex is reduced to the merely biological—when it is reduced, in fact, to the quest for orgasm—it becomes taking, not giving. Here is pure selfishness: personal expression, an impulse from within directed toward another, becomes mere self-directed physical stimulation.

Clearly the solution to this problem will not be a return to conventional morality in which physical exploitation was justified as long as the victim was one's spouse. To see the problem of sexuality—and the whole problem of relating intimately to others—in personalist terms reveals the mechanistic legalism of the conventional ethic. The conventional ethic, in viewing sex as something that happens only below the belt, gives young people no starting point for exploring its human dimension. The old view enslaved women by reducing them to their function, but women will not liberate themselves from that kind of slavery by abdicating their responsibility to decide "how far to go." Rather, it is necessary that men join them in making that decision. Indeed, the degree of intimacy is not as important as concern for the quality of the relationship.

Many young people have reached the point of asking themselves these questions. As in their political development, their first revolt was for more freedom, their second revolt was for greater responsibility. It is in this respect that this generation's revolt seems different from that of others. Every generation goes through its period of protest before settling down to the life its fathers planned for it. But this generation, having gone through the usual disenchantment, is demanding that there be something better to settle down to than what came before. Morals, politics and religion that seemed too strict in adolescence have revealed themselves as too lax in early adulthood. But it would be a mistake to write off this generation as puritanical because their personalist ethic is based on true regard for freedom.

THE ARTFUL REVOLUTION

One indicator of the sensibility of a generation is its attitude towards art. Art reflects the conscience of a generation. Where trends in thought are difficult to determine, trends in art often indicate which directions thought is following. It is my intention here to select a few relevant strands of modern art and to suggest their implications for the sensibility of my generation. These may not be the most important or obvious themes in contemporary art, but they represent the "flavor" of the age. Needless to say, this approach will be highly tendentious, but conclusions will be drawn in concrete terms and can therefore be judged on their descriptive accuracy alone.

Much of the art of recent years seems to reflect an increasing suspicion of the human dimension of things. Art was once a process of shaping materials in ways that introduced into their form an element of the personal, internal realm of men. Now man seems to have grown unsure of his grasp of that area. Today's artist has fallen back on the nature of materials themselves. In architecture, for example, a Gothic cathedral is a comment on the nature of man, not on the nature of stone. A steel and glass skyscraper manages to tell us only a little about steel and glass. Structures are formed not in terms of the human imagination but in the way the building materials suggest. The same tendency can be seen in the development of electronic music and even in computer poetry.

In each of these cases there is an attempt to let the material —whether metal, or sound, or words—virtually shape itself into the completed work. A mind, of course, must place the materials in some kind of order, but the intervention is as limited as possible. I view this as a result of an uneasiness on the part of artists, an unwillingness to trust their imaginations. Modern architecture is "clean" because it displays a minimum of human complication—a fact, not a demonstration of personality. I do not want to try to account fully for this backing away from the imagination. I only want to point out the trend. Once it is recognized, we can see evidence of it everywhere.

This kind of art not only avoids excessive entanglement with the creative imagination but with the imaginative enjoyment of the work of art as well. Thus the drift in many areas of art is toward greater and greater emphasis on externals and upon surfaces. When we think of contemporary interior decoration, for example, we think of bright objects against a white background, all evenly illuminated by fluorescent light. Such a room is surfaces, solid colors against solid colors. Materials that have depth, like wood, are increasingly replaced by materials that have only surface, like plastic and aluminum. For another example, the greatest innovation in theater in this century has been the introduction of Artaudian techniques, in which voice and gesture are heavily stressed and characterization almost eliminated. Again, the art revolves around the external, and shuns interior involvement with man himself.

It is easy to see how this tendency relates to what has happened to philosophy in this century. Positivism and linguistic analysis have insisted that we cannot generalize about man's spirit, but only judge whether or not what he says is logical. Behaviorism further emphasizes externals by replacing motivation from within with stimulation from without as an explanation for human behavior. The new art seems based on the behaviorist premise. It seeks not to stir man, not to evoke a response, but simply to stimulate him, to produce a predictable and undefined reaction. One might examine an impressionist or imaginatively abstract painting for any length of time, and derive more and more from the work with increasing study, but an op art painting, once seen, is fully perceived. The imagination can add nothing because it provides nothing to build on. Materials with depth can be examined from a hundred angles, in a hundred different lights, and be seen as different every time; while materials which are all surface, like plastic, provide no motive at all for second thoughts. Technological man surrounds himself with surfaces that reveal themselves completely, and which therefore render imagination irrelevant to their complete appreciation.

Let us assume without proving it that this trend represents the direction of the future, and is the culmination of various assumptions about man already implicit in our culture. We have been examining some of the ways that young people are in revolt against aspects of that culture. This decade has witnessed a revolutionary regeneration in the moral sensibility of young people and disgust and shame on their part over the slick moral relativism that has made racism, proverty and war continuing realities. The personalist vision of these students militates against the behavioristic determinism that characterizes much of their college education. Their intense sensitivity to social manipulation can be seen as a repudiation of the scientific and technological mentality that has taken hold in this age. In other words, young people are in opposition to precisely the forces in our culture that have promoted the trends in art that have just been described. We might expect that their cultural life style would reflect that opposition.

In some senses it clearly does. While their surroundings become more and more bland, young people are becoming more and more colorful. Their music and dress both reflect a heavy emphasis on imagination and variety. There has been an explosion of interest in personal vision which has led to the drug cult and the hippie phenomenon, among other things. Modern music—whether the sterile Broadway variety or the non-harmonic type composed by men like Cage—has drifted farther and farther away from the sensibility of real people, but music like that of the Beatles reasserts the humaneness of art by its unashamed indulgence in a whole range of human emotions and concerns. Rock music is founded upon a rhythm that is contagious precisely because it is the natural rhythm of the body, whereas the complex rhythms of much modern music are not.

The repudiation of the dehumanizing tendency in art has not been complete. At the heart of that trend is the replacement of expression from within by stimulation from without; and this confusion has in some ways poisoned the cultural milieu of young people as well as it has that of their parents. The prime example of this is the drug problem. The LSD craze is one of the strongest indications of the interest of youth in the imagination and its enhancement, but the whole drug cult is implicitly based on the materialist behaviorism it tries to surpass. Thus young people who take drugs think that spiritual insight can be gained by push-button, that it can be imposed from without. Another example is that stream of the sexual revolution that reduces sex to its biology, in which sex is merely stimulation, and not an expression of something that is felt. Rock music is prey to the same contagious tendency, which sometimes calls for volume so high as to make music physically stimulating by its sheer intensity.

All these kinds of stimulation are depersonalizing because they are manipulative. When art reduces itself to depthless surfaces, or to external stimulation, it is refusing to evoke a response from its audience, but is rather seeking to impose an effect upon it. The political and moral implications can be easily drawn. Student activists who seek a revolution in American society can choose one of two paths to change: they can effectively manipulate their opponents, or they can successfully change them. Art reflects the conscience of the age, and the changing trends in the artistic sensibility of young people might reveal earlier than their other activity the particular direction towards change which they will choose.

conclusion

student power and hope

All the conflicts between students and institutions, described in this book, question the allocation of power between them. Student viewpoints do not call attention to themselves merely by their existence, but because students are turning their ideas into programs for action. It is attempts at achieving change that have won so much prominence for the thinking of students. Demonstrations, confrontations with police and disruption on campuses are all aimed at winning a measure of power for activist young people and a position of influence for their points of view. Since the quest for power by students has generated much of the controversy that surrounds their public behavior, it is fitting to consider briefly some features of the power they seek.

Classically, the first element of freedom is power over one-self, that is, freedom from personal constraint. This ideal informs the original revolt of young people. Students of every generation have at some point in their careers fought for their right to think, speak and act freely, and my generation is no exception. The first murmurs of dissent in our high school days were directed at the restrictive atmosphere of the tradition in which we were being educated. This liberalism developed into a conviction that our principal political task was the assurance of political liberty for everyone in our society. This was the impulse behind our early involvement in the civil rights movement and the starting point of our whole political evolution.

The failure of the civil rights movement altered some of the premises which had inspired this struggle for personal freedom. Students emerged from that experience with more complex ideas of freedom. They saw that political liberty was not completely satisfying unless it was supported by economic freedom, racial equality, and so on. They not only had to be free to be themselves, but they had to have the power to create a life that was more than a life of slavery. Students who had at first been content to fight for their right to speak their minds in class now turned their energies toward reform of the educational system itself. They developed a new concern for the second aspect of power—power over environment. They directed their efforts towards others by working for solutions to poverty and civil rights problems.

This new emphasis makes this generation's revolt truly revolutionary. Every generation reaches a point where it petitions its elders for an advance on the power it expects to inherit in adulthood. The activists of the present generation have gone beyond this simple restlessness. They have begun to suspect that as adults they might not inherit real power at all, but that nearly everyone in a collectivized society is economically, socially and politically impotent. The developing nations of the world, with which students often identify, have made the same discovery. Their first goal was the end of colonialism. When colonialism was defeated, they realized that they were still effectively controlled by the larger nations. Students who used to imagine that reaching twenty-one would signal liberation know now that effective control by others will not be shrugged off so easily.

The first phase of student activism was addressed to those who hold power in our society—parents, teachers, the clergy, government. Students asked that a small measure of the power, which they thought everyone else possessed, be given to them. Then their experience of activism taught them that power was more elusive than that. Like black activists, they have now stopped asking for gifts of power, and they are trying to create their own. They feel capable of solving the problems that previous generations have not solved, and so they feel they deserve an effective role in public affairs. Cold War conflicts and racism, for example, grow upon the fears of many of our citizens. Student activists, whose work with blacks and with persons of all political shades has cured them of much of this fear of the different, feel liberated from the insecurity that plagues a great many people in America. Freedom from such fear permits them to effect a reconciliation with the powerless at home and abroad. This feeling of liberation from fear of oppressed minorities is at the heart of a student movement that is now international.

Some oppose the growth of real power in the hands of activist young people on the ground that students are attempting to control everything. No doubt some students might like to, but this is clearly not the posture of the movement as a whole. Youth cries, "Move over," not "Step down." They want to *share* the power not to take all of it. In this sharing of power, the skills of their elders would be tempered by the special insights of the activist experience. Of course, even this frightens those who imagine that most activists are at heart either anarchists or totalitarians. I hope that readers who have come this far do not share the fears of the establishment. Leaving them aside, the question remains whether the young, who have freed themselves of many of their fears, will use power in a way that recognizes the fears of others.

The danger that they will not—that the exercise of power by the young will destroy the sensitivity to others created by their original powerlessness—sometimes leads even sympathetic critics to wish that students would confine their ideas to the classroom. We are warned that power corrupts, and that idealism will not survive a recourse to "confrontation politics." Of course, the dangers must be acknowledged, but so must the weakness of the criticism. It is not realistic to expect that the passionate convictions of the young will not be mobilized in action. If those who have been converted to a new vision of the world remain mere visionaries, this will be a corruption of all that activism means. No one can effect change—indeed, no one should hope for it—who dares not risk the exercise of power. For although it may be true that power corrupts charity, it is more surely true that powerlessness corrupts faith and hope.